About the author

Jason C. Myers is Professor of Political Science at California State University, Stanislaus. He is the author of *Indirect Rule in South Africa*, as well as numerous articles on ideology and political theory.

Jason C. Myers

The politics of equality
an introduction

Zed Books
LONDON · NEW YORK

The politics of equality: an introduction was first published in 2010 by
Zed Books Ltd, 7 Cynthia Street, London N1 9JF, UK, and Room 400,
175 Fifth Avenue, New York, NY 10010, USA

www.zedbooks.co.uk

Set in Monotype Sabon and Gill Sans Heavy by Ewan Smith, London
Index: ed.emery@thefreeuniversity.net
Cover designed by Rogue Four Design

A catalogue record for this book is available from the British Library
Library of Congress Cataloging in Publication Data available

ISBN 978 1 84813 844 5 hb
ISBN 978 1 84813 843 8 pb
ISBN 978 1 84813 845 2 eb

Contents

Figures | vi
Acknowledgments | vii

Introduction 1
1 Historical materialism 6
2 Equal freedom 34
3 Economy and society 49
4 Democracy 83
5 Internationalism 108
6 The privation state 125
Conclusion 133

Notes | 135 Bibliography | 147
Index | 154

Figures

1.1 Stabilization of the US economy through government
     intervention 28
1.2 Shares of income received by US households by
     quintile, 1967–2005 29
1.3 Gini index of US income inequality, 1967–2005 29
1.4 US productivity and wages, 1980–2005 30
1.5 US labor union membership, 1970–2006 31
1.6 Work stoppages, 1970–2006 31
4.1 Gini index of income inequality, 2005 102

Acknowledgments

The inspiration for this book emerged from my experiences teaching college courses on political philosophy and ideology. Thanks, therefore, go to my students at the University of Cape Town and California State University, Stanislaus who helped me both to recognize the need for such a book and to sharpen my understanding of its subject. Thanks also go to Michael MacDonald, Michael Metelits, Michael Jon Olson, and Paul Thomas, who encouraged me to pursue the project and commented on the initial drafts. A sabbatical leave from California State University, Stanislaus in 2008 assisted tremendously in the completion of the final manuscript. Ken Barlow, Jakob Horstmann, and Ewan Smith at Zed Books guided the project through its final stages to publication.

Introduction

In late 2008, after decades of absence, the word 'socialism' suddenly reappeared in American political discourse. Candidate Barack Obama was labeled a socialist by his Republican Party opponents; soon President Obama would be denounced by protestors at anti-tax, anti-government 'Tea Party' rallies for leading the country toward socialism. The Socialist Party USA's national chairman published an editorial in the *Washington Post* denying that Obama was any kind of socialist, while the *New York Times* invited a group of scholars to debate the meaning of socialism today.[1]

To be sure, the political context in which that question might now be considered is murky and riddled with contradictions. In the People's Republic of China, a communist government promotes the development of privately owned businesses, permits the expansion of income inequality, and increasingly distributes goods such as education and healthcare according to market principles: those with the ability to pay receive what they want, others make do as they can. In the United States, as a severe economic crisis began in 2007, a self-described pro-business 'conservative' administration responded with a strategy not at all unlike the one suggested by Karl Marx and Friedrich Engels in the *Communist Manifesto*: the use of public resources and governmental authority to bring stability to an economy whipped into dangerously turbulent froth by the uncoordinated decisions of private investors.

The cable news critics and Tea Party protestors who charged that Barack Obama and the Democratic Party were engineering a socialist transformation of the United States pointed accusingly at the two most prominent features of the first-term president's policy agenda: passage of a healthcare bill that would extend insurance coverage to all Americans and government-led economic stimulus intended to pull the country's economy out of recession. Viewed from a wider historical perspective, though, the most surprising aspect of this furious debate was that it involved any substantial controversy at all. For most of the twentieth century, political momentum in the highly developed countries had been building toward a point at which the core values underlying national health insurance and government economic intervention appeared to be permanent features of the modern social landscape.

Consider, for example, the influential essay published in 1950 by British sociologist T. H. Marshall, arguing that over the long sweep of three centuries, citizens in the highly developed countries had gradually secured three generations of rights. The principle of equal legal rights had been won during the eighteenth century. In the nineteenth century, the rise of parliamentary government added political rights. Social rights – basic forms of material security and wellbeing such as education, healthcare, minimum incomes, and retirement pensions – would be the inevitable achievement of the twentieth century.[2]

The real historical processes through which citizen rights were won were never so neat and clean as this. The form of legal equality achieved in the eighteenth century was limited almost everywhere to men judged to belong to the proper racial category. Until the end of the nineteenth century, political rights in most countries with elected legislatures were granted only to those who could demonstrate ownership of a significant amount of land or financial wealth. Throughout the nineteenth and twentieth centuries, parties identifying themselves as socialist, communist, or social democratic argued and fought for political transformations that would secure material wellbeing and equality for working people in the industrialized countries. Wherever citizen rights of any kind were achieved, they were the result of protracted political struggles in which many lost their lives and whose outcomes were never guaranteed.

By the middle of the twentieth century, however, the momentum in favor of social rights was undeniable. Even in the United States, where self-described socialist, communist, or social democratic parties were never significant contenders in national elections, both major political parties felt compelled to adopt (or at least to accept) important elements of their policy agenda: the eight-hour workday, the minimum wage, collective bargaining rights, unemployment insurance, Social Security pensions. Anyone surveying the political landscape of the highly developed countries circa 1950 would surely have concluded, as Marshall did, that social rights were now permanent features of modern citizenship, as fundamental and unquestionable as equality before the law and electoral democracy.

Yet, some fifty years after the publication of Marshall's essay, social rights appeared to fall suddenly into retreat. Even in the richest of the highly developed countries, all discussion of education, healthcare, and retirement income concerned cutbacks and belt-tightening. This was not because of a general economic slowdown. In the United States, productivity expanded steadily and at times dramatically from 1980 to 2008. The shortage of public resources and the sudden scarcity of social rights were the result of political decisions explicitly aimed at reducing the level of taxes paid by businesses and wealthy individuals and reducing the bargaining power of organized workers. A small elite of business owners grew fabulously wealthy as the material position of ordinary working people stagnated and sank.

One way, then, in which to consider the question of social rights would be to study the historical trajectory of the organizations, parties, and movements that have declared themselves to be devoted to their achievement.[3] As important as this work is, however, the accounts of a party or movement's history are unlikely to tell us everything we might need to know about the ideas that inspired it or the logic behind its policy agenda. Socialist, communist, and social democratic parties, for example, have argued in favor of greater material equality, the expanded provision of public goods, and the use of government to guide economic development. But why? What, precisely, is hoped to be achieved by providing citizens with universal healthcare or education? Why do wealth and income inequality matter so much to the political left? Does equity matter on a global scale or should we only be concerned with the relative status of citizens within individual nation-states?

Questions like these take us on to the terrain of political philosophy. And while it may seem at times that what we encounter there is useful only for the purposes of armchair speculation or coffee shop debate, in fact political philosophy is ultimately inseparable from the concrete world of political action. Politics is the process through which human communities make decisions regarding their collective conditions of existence. But unless such decisions are to be made blindly, political actors must be equipped with understandings of the context in which they are situated and the goals they hope to achieve. These are what political philosophy has to offer. To the extent, then, that we seek to understand the world of politics or that we seek to sharpen our own ability to engage with that world, the study of political philosophy can benefit us.

The core values of socialist, communist, and social democratic political philosophy, though, have become obscured over the course of the nineteenth and twentieth centuries. The prominence of the broad socialist left in the modern era meant that by the middle of the twentieth century, its political philosophy often seemed self-evident. Little needed to be said about what socialists, communists, or social democrats stood for – the important questions concerned their tactics, strategies, and chances of success. The successes achieved by the movement meant that by the second half of the twentieth century, many elements of its policy agenda had been incorporated into the economic and political life of the industrialized countries. Yet the inability of Western socialists to overcome the powerful resistance of wealthy elites and organized business ultimately resulted in the stagnation of their movement and the transformation of their political philosophy into an increasingly arcane topic of study dealt with primarily by professional academics.[4]

The history of sectarian party competition deepened this problem. During the nineteenth century, the most common terms used to refer to a broad grouping of organizations and ideologies on the political left – socialist, communist, social democratic – were effectively interchangeable. As divisions between parties sharpened in the twentieth century, these terms came to stand for highly specific approaches to strategy or policy. Yet, as the same parties continued to evolve, the precise definitions of their positions (which can still be found in high school and college textbooks) became increasingly meaningless.

This book, then, has two immediate purposes. First, I have sought to clarify and rearticulate in contemporary terms the core values of socialist, communist, and social democratic political philosophy. It should be noted that in doing so, I have chosen to focus exclusively on the presence of these values in Western political thought. This has not been done out of a lack of regard for the importance of philosophical traditions originating in the East or in sub-Saharan Africa. Rather, I have chosen to put forward a work within my own range of specialist competency and to leave other areas to those better equipped to analyze and present them. Second, rather than continuing to parse distinctions between socialists, communists, and social democrats that are now often inaccurate or irrelevant, I have attempted to identify key elements of political philosophy that are shared within a broad tradition emphasizing the importance of social rights and social equality. Chapter 1 sets out the broad context for social egalitarian political philosophy by identifying its theory of history. Chapter 2 drills down to locate the core of social egalitarian political philosophy: its unique concept of equality. Chapter 3 explores the ways in which social egalitarians have sought to realize that ideal of equality through the organization of economic life. Chapter 4 examines the relationship between social equality and the practice of democratic politics. Chapter 5 describes the extension of egalitarian ideals across national boundaries in the theory and practice of internationalism. Chapter 6 discusses the challenge posed to the values of social equality by market fundamentalism at the end of the twentieth century.

Although much of this book will be concerned with history, it does not offer the reader a comprehensive history of social egalitarian political thought. The book proceeds thematically, rather than chronologically. In this respect, it looks through the past, toward the future. Organizations, parties, and movements rise and fall. Even the names by which people refer to political beliefs are subject to change. A self-identified 'conservative' in the United States today is unlikely to subscribe to the same ideals as a 'conservative' in France circa 1789. Certain core values, however, are more durable, moving between different historical contexts, in and out of formal institutions, finding expression under a variety of different headings. To this extent, the analysis provided here should prove useful not only to those interested in understanding political movements of the past, but to those seeking to understand the presence of social egalitarian values in politics today and in times to come.

ONE

Historical materialism

Perhaps unlike any other tradition of political philosophy, social egalitarianism has been conflated – and confused – with its theory of history: the analytic framework that attempts to explain, in a basic sense, how human societies function and how they change over time.

Most typically, that conflation and confusion occurred as part of the critical reaction to the work of Karl Marx. In total, Marx's body of scholarship comprises a theory of history, a critique of capitalism (including intertwined philosophical and economic aspects), and some limited speculation about economic and political pathways toward social equality. Yet, particularly during the twentieth century, critics tended to fix their attention on Marx's theory of history, reducing not only his work but the broad social egalitarian tradition as a whole to this solitary element. For Cold War-era scholars in the West, this was clearly a strategic choice. If the ideological battle between the United States and the Soviet Union could be reduced to a single question, it would be that much easier to land a knockout blow. Whether or not the mountain of books and articles produced by this effort had any real impact on the outcome of the Cold War is a question that need not detain us here. What we can say for certain is that the intensive critical focus on Marx's theory of history tended to create the impression that the uniqueness of social egalitarian political philosophy lay not in the specific nature of its theory of history, but simply in its *possession* of a theory of history. Social egalitarians (so the assumption ran) drew their political beliefs from a package of presumptions and speculations about historical change, while the adherents of other ideological traditions did not.

In fact, even a cursory examination of the history of political thought reveals that nothing could be further from the case. Consider, for example, the great debate in Western political thought between Thomas Hobbes and Jean-Jacques Rousseau. In 1651, Hobbes published his landmark text, *Leviathan*, in which he rigorously defended the legitimacy of monarchy, stressing that it was not divine right, but the ability to create peace and order which should lead us to respect and obey a sovereign.[1] Just over a century later, in his now equally famous *Social Contract*, Rousseau issued the scathing reply that peace and order could be found in jail cells, though this failed to make them any more desirable places to live.[2] At surface level, of course, this was a debate about the nature of legitimate authority. Could the power of a monarch to command an entire society be genuinely rightful? Or was sovereignty only truly legitimate if it involved the active participation of citizens? Beneath the surface, however, lay two competing theories of history. For Hobbes, the dynamics of social life and historical change could be traced to the fact that human beings generally were aggressive, acquisitive, and perfectly willing to do violence to one another in pursuit of their aims.[3] Only the clear, unified power of a monarch could guarantee law, order, and – most importantly for Hobbes – property rights.[4] For Rousseau, it was precisely the invention of private property which led to social conflict in the first place.[5] The key to social order, then, was not simply the defense of property rights, but the prevention of severe material inequality:

> Do you therefore want to give constancy to the State? Bring the extremes as close together as possible. Tolerate neither rich men nor beggars. These two estates, which are naturally inseparable, are equally fatal to the common good. From the one come the fomenters of tyranny, and from the other the tyrants. It is always between them that public liberty becomes a matter of commerce. The one buys it and the other sells it.[6]

The classical liberal explanations of property rights, political legitimacy, and economic organization are similarly framed within overarching theories of history. John Locke's *Second Treatise of Government* traces property rights to the biblical creation story and its suggestion of two original claims: a common right to the Earth, shared by all, and an exclusive right to one's body, held by the individual. Locke famously holds that as they do work, individuals combine their labor power with elements of the world, thereby establishing private claims to whatever their labor touches and transforms.[7] In *Wealth of Nations*, Adam Smith proposes that the historical development of economic relationships can be explained by a natural human propensity 'to truck, barter, and exchange one thing for another.'[8]

What, then, is the purpose of a theory of history for political philosophy? We might begin to answer that question by first reflecting on the nature of politics itself. Most fundamentally, politics is the range of processes through which we consciously shape the conditions for our collective existence. Politics, in other words, is centered on will and choice. If you believe that all events in the universe unfold according to a divine plan or a mechanical chain reaction in which human initiative plays no part, politics can be nothing other than a minor theatrical performance: emotionally moving, perhaps, but ultimately unconnected to the levers of power. If, however, human free will is real – if it is meaningfully possible to choose between alternate courses of action – then politics matters very much.

Choice, though, if it is not to be thoughtless or random, requires something to guide it. This, of course, is the job of political philosophy: to serve as a set of directions and criteria for political decision-making. But the specific directions to a destination can be formulated only in the context of broader knowledge about who and where we are. What are human beings? What, if anything, is our fundamental nature? What sort of world do we inhabit? How do the societies in which we find ourselves operate and how, if at all, do they change? It is entirely possible that we may not be capable of answering questions like these. It is surely possible that some of our answers may be wrong. But if we are able to say something both meaningful and truthful about who and where we are, it might then become possible to consider the range of political choices that are either consistent or inconsistent with the facts of our existence. This is the reason why we find theories of history at the heart of all traditions of political philosophy.

The materialist theory of history

It is by no means the case that all examples of social egalitarian political thought share precisely the same foundational theory of history. Yet, with respect to basic understandings of human existence and social change, the broad social egalitarian tradition contains some strong family resemblances: distinctive characteristics that allow us to recognize members of a related group, even when every member does not necessarily share every characteristic. I have chosen to refer to the theory of history whose most fundamental elements are commonly found in the work of social egalitarians as a materialist theory of history, despite the fact that this term brings with it a certain amount of controversy.

Just as with the terms used to identify social egalitarian programs and parties ('socialism,' 'communism,' 'social democracy'), both advocates and opponents have at times insisted on narrow and exclusive definitions of historical materialism, maintaining that the name should be applied only to one particular interpretation of one particular author's work. There is, of course, nothing wrong with political or scholarly debates over the correct interpretation of ideas. Neither politics nor scholarship could proceed without such exchanges. But it is also worth remembering that debates about the interpretation of an idea lose an important aspect of their meaning if we allow ourselves to view them only as the staunchest partisans do, seeing those on one side as the true bearers of a tradition and the others as infidels. Baptists and Mormons disagree with one another about the correct interpretation of Christian scripture. The most militant Baptist believers may even claim that Mormons are not truly Christians, or vice versa. An analysis of Mormonism, though, would go very badly wrong in beginning from the proposition that it was something other than an interpretation of Christianity. We should not be deterred, then, from recognizing the broad outlines of a materialist theory of history by the fact that some partisans (and some critics hoping to erect a convenient straw target toward which to direct their attacks) will seek to restrict all discussion of it to their preferred interpretation.

One important early version of a materialist theory of history is contained in Rousseau's *Discourse on the Origin of Inequality*, a text which opens by flagging for the reader's attention the central role to be played by a theory of history in the remainder of the argument: 'O man, whatever country you may be from, whatever your opinions may be, listen: here is your history, as I have thought to read it, not in the books of your fellowmen, who are liars, but in nature, who never lies.'[9]

The history that Rousseau proceeds to recount begins from the most fundamental relationship between human beings and their world. The human animal possesses, in a physical sense, both needs and abilities, and interacts with the material world in order to meet those needs.[10] Rousseau imagines the earliest human ancestors to have been solitary creatures, individually roaming the forests, searching for food, and meeting one another only occasionally in order to mate. Contemporary anthropological research would surely disagree with him on this point. The key element, though, of Rousseau's theory of history is not his belief that the earliest humans were non-social animals, but his recognition of a connection between the conditions under which we meet our basic physical needs and the possibilities for social and political organization.

Whether or not human beings began their historical existence in relative isolation from one another, like reptiles, they did not stay that way. But as he tries to account for the development of human social life, Rousseau encounters a puzzle. Could forms of social and political domination, like those in his own world of the eighteenth century, have existed among the earliest generations of human ancestors? When and how, in other words, did durable forms of inequality – servitude and slavery – become possible? The answer is not to be found in the natural distribution of strength or skill, but in the situational conditions within which strength and skill can be brought to bear:

> Some will dominate with violence; others will groan, enslaved to all their caprices. That is precisely what I observe among us; but I do not see how this could be said of savage men, to whom it would be difficult even to explain what servitude and domination are [...] Is there a man with strength sufficiently superior to mine and who is, moreover, sufficiently depraved, sufficiently lazy and sufficiently ferocious to force me to provide for his subsistence while he remains idle? He must resolve not to take his eyes off me for a single instant, to keep me carefully tied down while he sleeps, for fear that I may escape or that I would kill him [...] After all that, were his vigilance to relax for an instant, were an unforeseen noise to make him turn his head, I take twenty steps into the forest; my chains are broken, and he never sees me again for the rest of his life.[11]

The difference with Rousseau's world is clear. Under primitive conditions, twenty steps into the forest lead to unclaimed ground and free access to the resources necessary for survival. But the eighteenth-century American slaves who strike out for freedom flee into a world in which the land they might otherwise farm is marked by property lines and the tools they will need to pursue a trade are hoarded in stores, available only for cash. Servitude and slavery, then, become possible when some can be made materially dependent upon others. And material dependence, Rousseau suggests, is rooted in the control of necessary productive resources.

Such resources are also the central focus of Marx's theory of history, the best-known version of which is found in his 1859 Preface to the *Critique of Political Economy*:

In the social production of their life, men enter into definite relations that are indispensable and independent of their will, relations of production which correspond to a definite stage of development of their material productive forces. The sum total of these relations of production constitutes the economic structure of society, the real foundation, on which rises a legal and political superstructure and to which correspond definite forms of social consciousness. The mode of production of material life conditions the social, political, and intellectual life process in general. It is not the consciousness of men that determines their being, but, on the contrary, their social being that determines their consciousness. At a certain stage of their development, the material productive forces of society come in conflict with the existing relations of production, or – what is but a legal expression for the same thing – with the property relations within which they have been at work hitherto. From forms of development of the productive forces these relations turn into their fetters. Then begins an epoch of social revolution. With the change of the economic foundations the entire immense superstructure is more or less rapidly transformed.[12]

Like Rousseau, Marx identifies a connection between the development and control of productive resources and the historical transformation of social institutions. Two elements, however, stand out in Marx's 1859 encapsulation of historical materialism. First, the progressive development of productive forces takes center stage here in a way that it does not for Rousseau. The changing nature of technology is clearly important for Rousseau, but he sees its primary impact in the weakening of the human body. We grow physically weak in civilized society as we come to depend upon more and more powerful forms of technology.[13] Marx's 1859 Preface, though, connects technological development to the transformation of social institutions. Second, the specific nature of that connection is said to involve the rise of contradictions between productive forces and existing social relations, ultimately resulting in political transformation – revolution.

Yet it is precisely the political aspect of historical change which appears to be missing from the 1859 Preface. If the catalytic agent driving revolution was technological innovation, what role – if any – was played by political leadership, organizing, or even accidents of fate? Many during the twentieth century came to see the rigorously mechanistic view of technologically driven social transformation as

representative of both Marx's work and historical materialism generally, though this view always stood in sharp contradiction to the events
of Marx's life and to much of the rest of his writing.

The *Communist Manifesto* offers a perfect example of both. In
1847, Marx, along with his friend and co-author, Friedrich Engels,
had joined a small European political organization known as the
Communist League and they were asked to produce a short piece of
literature explaining the group's aims. This was not meant to be a
scholarly work, but an organizing pamphlet. Central Europe was on
the brink of revolution (which broke out in 1848 and swept through
nearly every country on the continent) and as he put himself into the
path of these events, Marx began his analysis of history not from
the question of technological development, but from the political
struggles surrounding social property relationships:

> The history of all society up to now is the history of class struggles.
> Freeman and slave, patrician and plebeian, lord and serf, guild-
> master and journeyman, in short, oppressor and oppressed stood in
> continual conflict with one another, conducting an unbroken, now
> hidden, now open struggle, a struggle that finished each time with
> a revolutionary transformation of society as a whole, or with the
> common ruin of the contending classes.[14]

Did Marx change his mind ten years after the failed revolutions
of 1848 and come to believe that technological development, rather
than political organizing, was the real key to social transformation?
Perhaps, although he remained active in revolutionary working-class
organizations throughout the remainder of his life, indicating that
he saw at least some important role to be played by politics. In any
event, the question is one that may be left to the Marxologists and
need not detain us here. It is enough for our purposes to note that
some examples of Marx's work suggest a theory of history focusing
on technological development and its related social contradictions,
while others center on political conflict and property relations.

At least one significant contemporary interpreter of Marx has
followed the former approach. G. A. Cohen has argued that Marx's
materialist theory of history is best understood as one in which
productive forces give shape to social relations. First come innovations in technologies and techniques, then, as a result, relationships
of ownership and control are reconfigured.[15] Other contemporary
interpretations of the materialist theory of history have followed

the latter approach. Ellen Meiksins Wood and George Comninel, for example, argue that broad social transformations in human history can best be understood as the outcomes of antagonism and struggle between those directly responsible for the production of social surpluses and those capable of extracting and expropriating surplus goods.[16] The economist Duncan Foley describes the materialist theory of history as focusing first and foremost on 'the real activities and relations of human beings rather than the revelation of divine will or the unfolding of the absolute idea.' More specifically, historical materialism explains the broadest and most important forms of change in human societies through their connection to 'the exact mechanisms through which ruling classes secured the control of surplus production, and the "contradictions" or instabilities [...] that these mechanisms implied.'[17]

What, then, are the basic common elements shared by these different approaches to a materialist theory of history? We can identify three. First, these are humanistic and material understandings of history, rather than theistic or metaphysical ones. They speak to us about the historical effects of human actions, decisions, and relationships in the context of a material world. They have nothing to say to us about the divine or the supernatural. Second, historical materialism begins its analysis of the human world from a recognition of the uniquely vital role played by productive activity. All human life depends upon regular, ongoing interaction with and transformation of the material world in which we find ourselves. Production in order to satisfy human needs and desires is central to social life and (materialist theories of history argue) shapes and influences all aspects of social life. Third, materialist theories of history recognize a fundamental causal connection between the organization of productive activity and the existence of social inequality. It is this insight which provides a potential link between historical materialism and social egalitarianism. To the extent that one is politically concerned with social inequality, the materialist theory of history offers an explanation of its origin and a basic suggestion as to where to turn to address it.

Of course, the simple fact that traditions of political philosophy contain and correspond to theories of history is no guarantee of the latter's validity. Rather than allowing truthful knowledge of our history and the world around us to influence our political beliefs, we could always work in the opposite manner: engineering a theory of history to fit whatever political beliefs we happened to hold. It should not be enough, then, simply to point out that social egalitarian political thought has typically rooted itself in a materialist theory of history. We must also enquire as to whether there is any evidence that this particular understanding of human history is scientifically accurate and not simply politically convenient.

Forces and relations

One place we might turn in the search for such evidence would be Jared Diamond's landmark study of human development, *Guns, Germs, and Steel*.[18] Diamond, a physiologist and geographer, opens his study with the sort of sweeping and pointed question that in another era might have come from a political philosopher like Rousseau. Why, he asks, did human beings on different continents develop such radically different forms of technology and social organization that some groups were able to conquer and dominate others? One possible answer suggests the existence of not just incidental but historically significant biological racial difference: Europeans possessed biologically determined forms of intelligence and technological ability that other 'races' lacked. Diamond, however, maintains that such racist explanations of technological development and imperialism are not simply distasteful, but demonstrably incorrect.[19]

Using a wide-ranging comparative method and incorporating data and analysis from several of the physical and social sciences, Diamond demonstrates that economic growth, technological innovation, political organization, and military prowess are fundamentally shaped by the nature of the physical environment in which human societies evolve.[20] First and foremost, the development of advanced technology, complex political organization, and a powerful military capacity depends upon the availability of large economic surpluses. Every person who spends a day experimenting with metal forging or tinkering with a tool in order to improve its efficiency does so at the expense of basic food production. Every person who serves in public office, in the military, or who educates those who do must be fed by others who spend their time producing food and other necessities. Only when a society's economic infrastructure is capable of producing more than enough basic goods to support all of its members does it become possible to take some people out of food production and allow them to engage in other activities. Further, some ways of making a living are more efficient than others. Most importantly, settled agriculture is far better at generating large surpluses than is hunting and gathering.[21]

Not all regions of the planet, however, are equally suited to the development of highly efficient food production systems. In order for a human community to make the shift from hunting and gathering to settled agriculture, the right combination of wild crops and domesticable animals must be available. Not all wild plants are equally fast growing and nutritious; not all large animals can be harnessed and trained to pull plows.[22] But in those places where the right combination of plants, animals, and weather conditions was available, a snowballing series of transformations took place. Large agricultural surpluses made larger populations possible. Larger populations brought with them the increased likelihood of conflict between strangers and increasingly difficult collective decision-making, especially with respect to issues such as economic allocation and spatial organization: who got what, when, and how. Thus, the shift in economic production from hunting and gathering to settled agriculture made the development of more complex forms of social and political organization not only possible, but also more likely. Diamond's study shows a strong correlation between economic structure, population size, and basic forms of government, from egalitarian bands or tribes to centralized states.[23]

Three aspects of Diamond's study, then, offer support to the materialist theory of human history. First, Diamond demonstrates the primacy of production not only to human existence, but to the developmental pathways available to human societies. Second, his study establishes the existence of a causal connection between the organization of production and wider forms of social and political hierarchy. Third, Diamond locates the key to that connection in the production and control of economic surpluses.

With these three points staking out the broad terrain of a scientifically demonstrable understanding of human history, we can now specify two critical elements at the core of such an understanding. The productive activities upon which human life depends are themselves dependent upon the availability of productive forces. We can include within this category natural resources, forms of technology, and human labor power. Productive forces, however, must be put to work within the context of specific human relationships. All productive activity is ultimately social. Adam Smith offers perhaps the best illustration of this axiom in *Wealth of Nations* as he unravels the complex division of labor required to produce an ordinary worker's cheap wool coat: shepherds, dyers, spinners, weavers, merchants, traders, shipbuilders, rope-makers, miners, bricklayers, and so on.[24] To the extent that a shipwrecked Robinson Crusoe carries even a knife with him to his deserted island, the productive activity he engages in remains connected to and dependent upon the work of others.

But in such a complex division of labor, how are the various tasks to be assigned? In the most basic sense, we could begin to answer that question by citing the unusual ability of human beings as a species to engage in self-reflection and behavior modification through the use of language. All the way back to Aristotle, philosophers and social scientists have noted the fact that human social organization appears to be the product of conscious agreement, rather than innate instinct.[25] Even contemporary sociobiologists who might reject such a *tabula rasa* portrait of human cognition would still be forced to admit that whatever social instincts we do possess cannot in themselves account for the tremendous variation in economic, cultural, and political institutions seen throughout history. Social variations like these cannot be explained in biological terms alone. They must involve at least some elements of convention or agreement.

With respect to divisions of labor, those forms of convention or agreement are chiefly concerned with the ownership and effective control of productive forces.[26] Who is able to exclude others from access to land, tools, or raw materials? Who is able to direct the labor of others? Who is able to appropriate economic surpluses from those directly responsible for producing them? The answers to questions like these tell us about the social relations of production through which forces of production operate. A piece of agricultural land, for example, might be farmed under the legal regime of European feudalism: owned by a member of an aristocratic elite (who could assume control of it through inheritance, marriage, or warfare) and worked by serfs legally required to turn over their surplus crops to the owner of the land. The same piece of ground brought into the world of contemporary capitalism might be owned by an individual or a corporation (who would most typically assume control of it through purchase) and any crops grown on it would likewise belong to the owners of the land. The labor needed to grow the crops, however, would now become an object of contractual exchange rather than legal obligation.

There are also other possibilities. Which among them will be selected at any given time, in any particular society, is the central problem addressed by historical materialism. On the one hand, relations of production are clearly variable enough to remove them from the list of behaviors governed entirely by biological instinct. On the other hand, though, the variations in productive relations throughout human history are not so random or chaotic as to suggest a field of entirely unconstrained possibilities. As we have seen, Marx's 1859 Preface proposed one possible model of a causal relationship between forces and relations of production. According to this hypothesis, forces of production shape relations of production. The 1859 Preface suggests this in two ways. First, it states that a society's relations of production correspond to a certain level of development of its productive forces. Second, it holds that the ongoing development of productive forces eventually pulls them out of sync with the relations of production, leading to crisis and revolution.[27]

There is also a wider claim involved here. Marx's 1859 Preface suggests a causal relationship connecting not only forces and relations of production, but the economic structure of a society and its legal, political, and cultural 'superstructure.'[28] Why, if relations of production are already molded by productive forces, would such an expansive superstructure be necessary? Relations of production involve the ownership and control of valuable resources. Wherever ownership is not egalitarian, the division of labor determined by the relations of production – and the distribution of benefits derived from productive activity – will be hierarchical. Feudal lords in their castles enjoyed every conceivable luxury available in their day, while the direct producers of the agricultural surpluses that made such a lifestyle possible lived very near the level of bare subsistence. In 2006, the average chief executive officer of an American corporation received 364 times the pay of an average worker.[29] Such uneven divisions of labor and reward might be maintained by coercive force, but as Rousseau reminds us, this can only be temporary: 'The strongest is never strong enough to be master all the time, unless he transforms force into right and obedience into duty.'[30] As G. A. Cohen puts it, economic systems require superstructures because might without right is inefficient and unstable.[31]

Just as with the general theory of historical materialism, though, we must ask whether there is evidence to support this hypothetical causal relationship between productive forces, productive relations, and social superstructures – or counter-evidence to oppose it. Diamond's study suggests a strong correlation between the change from hunting and gathering to settled agriculture and the shift from relatively egalitarian to highly centralized forms of government.[32] Correlation, of course, is not the definitive proof of causation, but it is the foundation of such proof. We can make a stronger claim for the proposition that productive forces shape productive relations and social superstructures by noting the conspicuous lack of counter-examples to the type of correlations Diamond focuses on. Hunting and gathering societies, for example, are characterized by highly informal and egalitarian relations of production, tending to lack any concept of the ownership of land and having relatively free access to necessary tools and materials. Nowhere do we find such productive relations surviving the introduction of settled agriculture and power-driven machines. Many pre-colonial African societies were effectively stateless, having no formal institutions of government or authoritarian leadership figures.[33] Nowhere do we find stateless societies after the Industrial Revolution.

Yet there is also an intriguing piece of counter-evidence to what Cohen has called the technological interpretation of historical materialism[34] in the fact that similar productive forces can be seen historically to correspond with very different productive relations and social superstructures. The ancient Greek city-states of Athens and Sparta, for example, did not differ with respect to the forces of production on which their economies were based. They existed in the same region of the world, enjoyed the same mild Mediterranean climate, and possessed the same range of food crops and domesticated animals. Both societies had the same knowledge of ceramics and metalworking. Their economic structures, however, differed radically. Athens was a slave-owning society, but the core of its agricultural production was carried out by free peasants, laborers, and tenant farmers.[35] Spartan agriculture, by contrast, was based entirely on a form of serfdom. A class of helots (who made up the vast majority of Sparta's total population) was strictly segregated from the city-state's citizen elite and legally required to produce and surrender the agricultural surpluses that fed their masters.

Politically, Sparta was a deeply conservative society, maintaining the same form of constitution for over four hundred years. Government rested in the hands of two hereditary kings and a council of thirty elders, appointed for life after the age of sixty. Literary, theatrical, or artistic activity was essentially nonexistent. Spartan citizens were expected to spend their time exclusively training for war. In these respects, Athens was Sparta's precise opposite. Rounds of significant constitutional change occurred every hundred years or so from the seventh to the fifth century BCE. By the 400s BCE, Athens had developed a form of government in which sovereign power was held by a popular assembly and public offices were assigned by random lot. The city's cultural output – particularly the work of its philosophers and playwrights – was unmatched in this era.

A similar comparison could be drawn between the United States and the Soviet Union. Admittedly, this case presents a potentially critical difference in the onset of industrialization: early in the USA; famously late in pre-revolutionary Russia. Yet, by the middle of the twentieth century, both societies had access to broadly similar resources and technology: large arable landmasses, steel, and power-driven machinery. Certain differences in the two countries' levels of economic development could no doubt be attributed to the timing of industrialization. But the radical divergence in their relations of production and social superstructures cannot be attributed solely to the development of productive forces, without also accounting for the political path taken by the Russian Revolution. The government brought to power in 1917 eventually embarked on a crash program of industrialization, but its leaders were not technicians or laboratory researchers struggling to develop new machines or chemical compounds. The Revolution did not create new forces of production, it transformed the relations of production, allowing existing productive forces to be used in new ways.

What both of these comparisons suggest is a less rigidly mechanistic model of social change, in which forces of production can be seen to determine a range of possibility for productive relations and superstructures. On the one hand, some forces and relations of production are incompatible with one another. The productive forces of mechanized manufacturing, for example, are clearly incompatible with the highly informal productive relations of hunter-gatherer societies. A contemporary automobile or computer factory would be unable to function without clear concepts of ownership, control, and division of labor. Who would be responsible for maintaining the machinery? Who would organize the inflow of raw materials? Who would determine the work schedule? Who would control, dispose of, and benefit from the finished products? Anarchists may protest that factory workers themselves could collectively agree on these matters – and indeed, they could. In order for production to go on in a contemporary industrial facility, critical questions could be decided collectively, but not informally. The workers at a chemical plant could organize their work schedule democratically, but they could not come and go as they pleased. Safety procedures could be drawn up jointly or by elected committees, but no worker could operate according to an unwritten, privately held sense of how things should be done. Hunting and gathering can be carried out successfully without formal rules and procedures, but large-scale mechanized manufacturing cannot.

Something similar can be said about the productive forces of advanced technology and the productive relations of slavery. The level of education and cultural sophistication required by, for example, computer technology would make the relations of slavery increasingly difficult to maintain over time.[36] High technology – both hardware and software – is delicate and easily sabotaged by workers driven by whips. It is true that during World War II, Nazi Germany used slave laborers in its V2 missile factories. Sabotage, however, was common, and it is difficult to imagine such a productive regime persisting for very long. Generally speaking, the productive relations of slavery have been compatible over long periods of time only with relatively primitive productive forces: basic agricultural tools, picks, shovels, and hammers.

On the other hand, most forms of productive technology are clearly compatible with more than one set of productive relations. The forces of production at work in a manufacturing plant could be privately owned by a single individual and operated by wage-earning employees. The same workforce could be employed to operate machinery owned not by a single individual, but by a collective group of shareholders. Under yet another set of productive relations, the shareholders and owners might be the workers themselves. Or the forces of production could be publicly owned and managed by a branch of government. Real-world examples of each of these possibilities are not difficult to find. Importantly, though, each represents a very different relation-ship between the members of a society and that society's productive forces. Each set of productive relations will offer different forms of control over labor time, working conditions, and the distribution of economic surpluses.

But if the level of development of a society's productive forces demarcates a range of possibility for productive relations – ruling out some, leaving others open – what selects between the available pathways? Why Athens with its peasant citizens and Sparta with its helots? Why the relatively small number of publicly owned enterprises in the United States and the relatively large number in Sweden? The answer in every case is the historically contingent process of political struggle. Nothing predetermined the victory of Franklin Roosevelt over Herbert Hoover in the 1932 US presidential election. But because of the outcome of that election, significant changes occurred in the productive relations of the American economy: workers gained rights to collective bargaining, publicly owned enterprises were developed, economic surpluses were distributed in the form of social benefits. The powers of politics are not unlimited. The availability of resources and technology exerts inescapable shaping forces on human societies and restricts the range of political choice. To the extent, though, that meaningful choices remain on the table, politics still has a role to play in determining the course of human history.

The materialist theory of history, then, suggests that productive forces broadly determine the development of human societies, pushing them in certain directions and blocking off others. Within the realm of the materially possible, political struggles will decide which path is taken and which left behind. But historical materialism also has something to say about the nature of those political struggles and their likely combatants. First and foremost, they will be class struggles.

Class and class struggles

Scholars have battled for decades over the proper definition of class and its social and political significance.[37] Still, the social sciences, popular literature, and ordinary discourse remain littered with vaguely defined uses of the term. Typically, these tend in one of two directions: rough indicators of wealth or equally imprecise indicators of social status. Edward Bellamy, whose 1888 novel *Looking Backward* imagined a twenty-first-century America thoroughly revolutionized by social egalitarianism, referred to four classes in the old world: the rich, the poor, the educated, and the ignorant.[38] Just over half of all Americans self-identify as members of the 'middle class.'[39]

Historical materialism's focus on the particular significance of productive relations, however, provides us with the basis for a more precise definition of class. Two key elements that we have already seen lead to that definition. First, the materialist theory of history identifies surplus production as especially critical in the organization and development of human societies. Second, historical materialism focuses its analysis on the specific social rules that organize the production and distribution of economic surpluses. As Diamond's study suggests, a deep and fundamental dividing line runs between the forms of society in which basic productive resources can and cannot be monopolized. Hunter-gatherers, having no ability to restrict access to the basic sources of food, clothing, and shelter, tend to live in informally organized, egalitarian bands. Once a society begins to practice settled agriculture, though, access to the land can be controlled. It then becomes possible – and typical – for productive resources to be monopolized by some at the expense of others.[40]

This fundamental economic relationship provides the basic criterion for historical materialism's definition of class. Positions in a class structure are determined by the ownership of significant productive resources, or the lack thereof.[41] It is important to note that this is an objective, rather than a subjective, definition of class. To the extent that the materialist theory of history focuses on the nature of social relations of production, it is possible to identify positions within such relations that exist independently of the perceptions of their participants. Someone in an alcohol-induced stupor may be a passenger in a car while completely unconscious or while believing him- or herself to be at home in bed. Nonetheless, a person standing on the street corner could watch the car as it passes and identify the passenger's objective position, regardless of what he or she believes it to be. Similarly, the participants in a class structure possess objective characteristics, whether or not they consciously self-identify with the descriptions of those characteristics produced by outside observers.

Most crucial among those characteristics is the ownership or lack of significant productive resources. Not only does this set of facts tell us about particular individuals, their class positions, and the ways in which they are likely to get along in the world, it tells us about the nature of their economic relationships with others. Those who are able to assert control over significant productive resources by means of social rules of ownership will be able to control the conditions under which those who lack such resources are able to make their living. The rules of property ownership within systems of slavery, feudalism, and capitalism differ radically. Slaves can be bought and sold by their masters, unlike serfs and wage laborers. Wage laborers have no legal obligation to work for any particular employer, unlike serfs or slaves. Yet slave masters, feudal lords, and capitalist employers share a fundamental similarity in their ability to control the labor of others.

The possibility of such control is given by the nature of a society's productive resources and its predominant forms of economic activity. Some types of resources and some forms of economic activity are more easily monopolized than are others. Agricultural fields are more easily monopolized than is unplowed forest or the open sea. Machine tools are more easily monopolized than are hand tools. Factories and retail stores are more easily monopolized than is arable land in a society with an open frontier. And where access to productive resources and the predominant forms of economic activity can be restricted, those who find themselves on the wrong side of the gate are likely to become dependent upon those who hold the keys.

One way to see this – and to reflect on the nature of economic dependence within a developed society – is with a brief thought experiment. Imagine being banned from working in any commercial enterprise, shopping in any retail store, or trading with anyone who still has the rights to engage in either activity. How would you survive? The conditions of life for the homeless in large American cities suggest one possibility: foraging for subsistence through the objects no longer claimed as pieces of private property – the trash. Better possibilities are not easy to imagine. It is difficult to say where one could find enough unclaimed arable land on which to grow subsistence crops and more difficult still to foresee the average member of a developed, urban society making a rapid transition from wage labor in a manufacturing or service industry to subsistence agriculture. The forms of dependence produced by the monopolization of productive resources are not without some qualifications and loopholes, but for most people, most of the time, they are very real and effectively inescapable.

It is also the case that in the forms of class society most familiar to us in history, those who are able to monopolize necessary productive resources are able to claim disproportionately large shares of the economic surplus. This is easiest to see in economic systems involving slavery or serfdom, but sometimes becomes muddied in the increasingly complex world of contemporary capitalism. For example, in a large, diverse economy like that of the USA, we could surely find owners of small businesses earning less in profits than some highly skilled and highly compensated employees earn in wages. Yet this could not be true within the same firm. Apart from financially independent hobbyists, the owners of small, marginally successful restaurants do not stay in business unless they earn more in profits than their cooks and waiters take home in wages.

A similar point can be made with respect to the profits of corpora-tions, whose owners are a diverse collection of stockholders. In 2008, US corporations reported earning over $1.5 trillion in profits.[42] We cannot tell from this figure, though, precisely how many shareholders divided up that sum or how much each individual shareholder re-ceived. It is hypothetically possible that if shares of stock in American corporations were divided equally between the country's 300 million citizens, each would receive only about $5,000 for the year. In fact, in 2001, 67.5 percent of financial wealth was owned by the richest 5 percent of all households. The richest 1 percent of all households owned 39.7 percent of all financial wealth. The bottom 40 percent of all households owned no financial wealth at all.[43] While some individual stockholders own more than others, in the aggregate, corporate stock – and corporate profits – are highly concentrated within a small elite.

Because so much is at stake in the relations of production – control of necessary resources, the ability to earn a living, the possibility of tremendous wealth – we should not be surprised by the conflictual nature of class relations. And while the term may strike our ears as distinctly modern, the recognition of class struggle as a key dynamic in political life can be traced back at least as far as the fifth century BCE. Plato's *Republic*, for example, contains several significant references to simmering class conflict in ancient Athens. Early in the text, the sophist Thrasymachus is depicted as arguing that justice can only be understood in the context of social divisions and struggles for power:

> Well, each government frames laws for its own advantage, a
> democracy for democrats, a tyranny for tyrants, and so on. In so
> legislating, the rulers represent this – their own advantage – as jus-
> tice for their subjects, and anyone who breaks their laws is punished
> as a lawbreaker and a criminal. Therefore I contend that justice is
> the same thing in every state: the advantage of the established ruling
> class.[44]

Later, as Socrates sketches out his imaginary city, it becomes clear that his proposed political institutions are specifically designed to prevent the sort of class struggle that drove ancient Athenian politics. On the one hand, Plato's Socrates presents a scathing critique of working-class power in the Athenian democracy, likening citizens attending the assembly to mutinous sailors who have seized control of a ship, despite the fact that none of them knows how to steer it.

On the other hand, though, Socrates' imaginary city is to be governed by a highly educated elite who, while holding an exclusive claim to political power, will live like soldiers and be strictly forbidden from possessing any private property.[45] The fact that Aristotle, too, recognized class struggle to be a key dynamic in ancient Greek political life can be seen, first and foremost, in his contention that democracy was not so much a particular set of institutions or practices (as we tend to think of it today) as a form of class rule: democracy was government by and for the poor. He goes on in *The Politics* to recount numerous instances of social upheaval, political reform, and revolution driven by conflict between classes identifiable by their possession or lack of property.[46]

Several centuries later, the early modern political philosophers remained in agreement with the ancients that the control of property lay at the root of social division and political conflict. For Hobbes, the likelihood of conflict over property rights was so great that all claims to such rights were effectively meaningless in the absence of a sovereign state capable of defending them against challenges.[47] Locke rejected Hobbes's reliance on the state for the establishment of basic property rights, but still found the defense of property claims to be the state's central legitimate purpose.[48] James Madison's assessment of the dangers facing society and government is even more strikingly clear about the matter:

> So strong is this propensity of mankind to fall into mutual animosi-
> ties, that where no substantial occasion presents itself, the most
> frivolous and fanciful distinctions have been sufficient to kindle their
> unfriendly passions, and excite their most violent conflicts. But the
> most common and durable source of factions, has been the various
> and unequal distribution of property. Those who hold and those who
> are without property, have ever formed distinct interests in society.[49]

Marx and Engels may now be perceived as having advanced a radical new position with their claim that the dynamics of political life were tied to and defined by the forces of class struggle. In fact, their assessment served only to put sharper emphasis on a point that was neither new, nor particularly controversial.

What would become increasingly contested over the course of the twentieth century was the suggestion that a revolutionary transformation of society by class conflict was historically inevitable. Whether or not Marx's work should be interpreted to mean this, the large

western European socialist parties that emerged near the end of his life adopted and propagated the idea. In the version of historical material-ism that would become familiar to scholars and political activists for decades to come, revolutionary transitions between historical stages of social development were brought about by technological change and the onset of economic crisis. Technological innovation was essen-tially inevitable, as were economic crises and, therefore, the political organization and mobilization of a revolutionary working class.[50]

There were good reasons to believe that this was true. The takeoff phase of the Industrial Revolution had dramatically transformed life in western Europe and the United States, creating vast new industries and the mass urban working class that made them run. Yet, with the same regularity with which the increasingly global economy produced new inventions and consumer goods, it also generated economic crises. A sharp recession preceded the European revolutions of 1848. A longer depression affected western Europe and the United States from the early 1870s to the middle 1890s. Recession and hyperinflation followed World War I, anticipating the Great Depression of the 1930s. Bank panics were intermittent throughout the period. Simultane-ously, trade unions and socialist parties grew larger and more potent. Between 1876 and 1905, mass socialist parties were founded in all of the industrialized European states. By 1916, they had made their presence felt in parliamentary elections. The most successful among them – the German and Scandinavian parties – could confidently look forward to a day when they would win electoral majorities.[51]

The central problem, of course, for a political movement premised on the idea of its own inevitability was the role of political activity itself. Did organizing matter or would workers become conscious of their class position and interests on their own? In practice, no mass socialist party simply sat on its hands, waiting for the arrival of economic crisis and revolution. But the question of class struggle's in-evitability hung on, primarily with academics. And as socialist parties in the highly developed countries first slowed their progress, then fell into retreat in the last decades of the twentieth century, the materialist theory of history came under broad attack. By the 1980s, the urban working class had become less homogeneous, less politically cohesive, and less interested in a transformation of capitalism.[52] As socialist parties lost ground, trade unions lost membership, and socialist ideo-logy fell out of fashion, nothing about class struggle or revolution seemed inevitable. Conservative commentators criticized historical materialism for predicting the downfall of capitalism, while a new generation of postmodernist scholars attacked what they deemed the Enlightenment view of human history as unfailingly progressive.

The critique of historical materialism centered on Marx's thought and introduced as evidence for the prosecution texts such as the 1859 Preface and Friedrich Engels's famous eulogy comparing the work of Marx and Darwin: the latter had discovered the laws of natural biological development; the former had discovered the laws of human historical development.[53] At the end of the twentieth century, as market economies flourished and socialist parties fell into retreat, the claim that the materialist theory of history was on a par with evolutionary biology – scientifically verifiable, accurate, and capable of revealing law-like dynamics of change – made a richly inviting target for critics in a variety of scholarly disciplines. Historical materialism predicted that technological development would produce economic crises, which in turn would lead to revolution. Capitalism's own development would automatically bring about its transformation into a new form of social life.

Far too few critics of the materialist theory of history have confronted the fact that, in reality, this is not far from what actually happened. The severe economic turbulence of the late nineteenth and early twentieth centuries – the grinding depressions, bouts of hyperinflation, and mass unemployment – ended in the highly developed countries only after significant alterations were made to the relationships between government, industry, and the financial sector. Laissez-faire capitalism produced the Great Depression, which in turn led to the political mobilization of workers (primarily in trade unions and the Communist Party), and government regulation of the economy. Figure 1.1 shows the effect of this transformation in the USA. Prior to the introduction of strong government intervention (primarily the regulation of banking and finance, management of interest rates, and propping up of consumer demand through job creation and income support), the economy swung wildly between periods of growth and decline. The relatively modest business cycle now experienced by the highly developed economies is not the product of pure, unadulterated capitalism, but a hybrid economic form, itself the result of crisis and political struggle – just what a materialist theory of history would have predicted.

The scientific status of historical materialism, however, has not only been underestimated, it has often been fundamentally misunderstood.

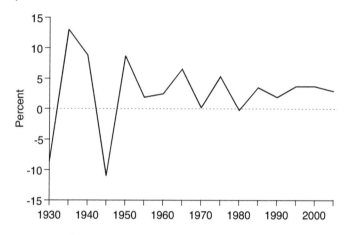

FIGURE 1.1 Stabilization of the US economy through government intervention
Source: US Department of Commerce, Bureau of Economic Analysis

The materialist theory of history possesses relatively strong explanatory power, but a significantly weaker predictive capacity. Ironically, it is this relative lack of predictive power which makes Engels's analogy between historical materialism and evolutionary biology perfectly appropriate and correct. As Stephen Jay Gould has pointed out, the theory of evolutionary biology is capable of explaining why living organisms possess certain characteristics, but it cannot predict the path of future evolutionary change.[54] Evolutionary biology holds that random mutations occasionally turn out to be useful for survival in a given environment. Organisms with characteristics that increase the chances of survival and reproduction pass those characteristics to their offspring. Useful characteristics are thereby propagated and detrimental characteristics weeded out. But the fact that a particular biological characteristic would be useful is not enough to produce it. The appearance of biological characteristics depends on random genetic mutation, which may or may not occur.

In much the same way, the materialist theory of history is able to explain why certain relations of production have come about and how they work. But it cannot predict with any degree of accuracy how or when future changes in the relations of production will occur. Revolutionized forces of production can put pressure on existing relations of production, but a society can reject or simply fail to adopt new technology.[55] Economic crises can precipitate political struggles, but the outcome of political contests – like the outcome of wars – is

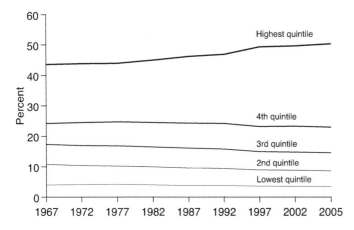

FIGURE 1.2 Shares of income received by US households by quintile, 1967–2005 *Source*: US Census Bureau, Historical Income Tables A-3

always uncertain. Thus, as historian Eric Hobsbawm points out, the general theory of historical materialism suggests the appearance of a succession of different modes of production, not the appearance of particular modes at particular times.[56]

Consider, for example, some key indicators of change in the US economy during the latter half of the twentieth century. Beginning in the 1980s, income inequality increased significantly (Figures 1.2 and 1.3). What caused this sudden transfer of wealth from one section

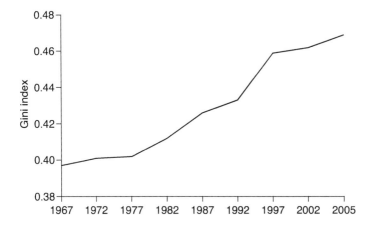

FIGURE 1.3 Gini index of US income inequality, 1967–2005 *Source*: US Census Bureau, Historical Income Tables A-3

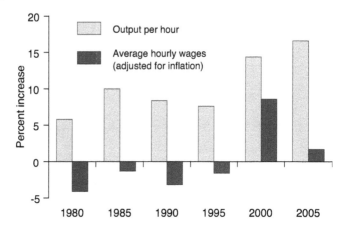

FIGURE 1.4 US productivity and wages, 1980–2005 *Source*: US Census Bureau, Statistical Abstract of the United States 2008, 1995, 1985

of the population to another? The possibility that American workers – particularly those in the lower income brackets – simply lost their sense of motivation and refused to work hard enough to earn high incomes is refuted by the facts. During the same years in which income was redistributed from the lower and middle strata to the top, the productivity of American workers increased steadily. Their wages, however, failed to keep pace, falling through the 1980s and early 1990s, and rebounding only modestly in the late 1990s (Figure 1.4).

What else changed during the 1980s and 1990s? The power of trade unions declined dramatically. Both membership in unions and the number of work stoppages they engaged in reached record low levels at the same time that the distribution of income shifted to favor the wealthy (Figures 1.5 and 1.6). The materialist theory of history would explain this confluence of events as the result of class struggle. During the 1980s, business owners and their political allies launched a successful assault on organized labor, the result of which was a significantly weakened labor movement and a redistribution of wealth from workers to employers.[57]

The materialist theory of history, then, can provide us with a powerful and accurate explanation of certain critical events. In a very broad sense, it predicts that those who own necessary productive resources and those who must seek out wage labor to make their living will struggle over control of the work process and distribution of the wealth it generates. But it cannot tell us who will win such contests.

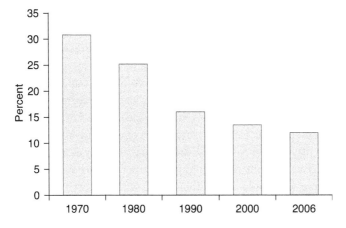

FIGURE 1.5 US labor union membership, 1970–2006 *Source*: US Census Bureau, Statistical Abstract of the United States 2008, 1985

The rise and fall of workers' organizations, the success or failure of political parties, and the introduction and effects of government policy remain outside the scope of historical materialism's predictive powers.

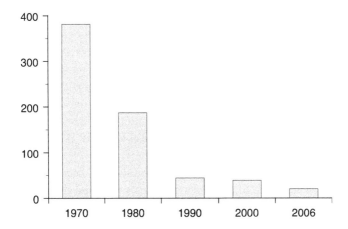

FIGURE 1.6 Work stoppages, 1970–2006 *Source*: US Census Bureau, Statistical Abstract of the United States 2008, 1985

Historical materialism and political philosophy

Given both its abilities and limitations, what is the usefulness of the materialist theory of history to social egalitarian political philosophy? In answering this question, we should first recall the purpose of theories of history for political philosophy generally. Political philosophy can be thought of as providing us with a set of directions for political decision-making. To the extent that we have meaningful choices to make about our collective way of life, various schools of political philosophy will indicate the correct turns to be made at particular junctions. Directions, though, must be plotted on a larger map of the terrain across which one intends to travel. This is the role played by theories of history. They instruct us as to the nature of ourselves and our surroundings, telling us where we could go, but not where we should go. In this sense, with respect to its ability to orient political philosophy, the lack of a robust predictive capacity is not a particularly serious weakness for a theory of history. We do not consult a map like an oracle, expecting it to reveal in advance the route we will travel on some future journey.

Three features of the landscape mapped by historical materialism are of central importance for social egalitarian political philosophy. First, the materialist theory of history suggests that we have meaningful choices to make about the nature of productive relations within our societies. Interestingly, with respect to this question, it is Adam Smith who proposes that our range of possibilities is constrained by a form of historical inevitability. If, as Smith claims, human beings possess innate drives to become economic specialists and to exchange with one another, societies of economic generalists with very limited trade relationships would be impossible. In fact, we know that many such societies have existed in the past and that a small number remain in existence today. By contrast, the materialist theory of history holds that the nature of our forces of production establishes a range within which we may choose politically between different possible relations of production.

Second, historical materialism suggests that because productive relations form the foundations of human societies, they will tend to influence much of what goes on in the rest of social life. The types of artistic production that appear in societies whose predominant productive relations are capitalist will tend to differ from those in feudal or small-scale hunting and gathering societies. Historical materialism can offer a powerful interpretive framework for artistic narratives.[58] Yet, like any such interpretive system, it has its limits. A materialist theory of history is not capable of predicting or even explaining every plot twist in a Hollywood screenplay or the director's choice of lighting for a particular scene. Artistic choices, forms of religious practice, and the dynamics of personal relationships will be powerfully influenced by a society's prevailing mode of production, but not completely determined by it.

Third, the materialist theory of history tells us that because we have choices to make about the nature of productive relations, and that those choices will affect (among other things) distributions of wealth and leisure time, we should anticipate conflict between those who stand to gain or to lose. Some of these conflicts will take place at the immediately economic level, within the workplace; others will be fought out in the political realm.

Social egalitarian political philosophy takes a partisan position with respect to such battles. But it is a partisan position that differs from others we might imagine. On the one hand, social egalitarians have consistently argued and fought for the interests of workers – those excluded from control of the means of production. What they have argued and fought for, though, is not a turning of the tables, but the creation of meaningful social equality. It is to the nature of that vision of equality that we turn next.

TWO

Equal freedom

In 2010, as the US political scene was roiled by vigorous – at times vicious – debate over a proposed public health insurance plan, the virtues of equality and freedom were routinely pitted against one another. Supporters of European-style national healthcare argued that it would rectify the persistent inequality between those in American society who had access to health insurance and those who did not. Their opponents strenuously maintained that such equality could be had only at the cost of freedom – a cost they deemed too high to pay.

We might reasonably assume, then, that social egalitarians are simply those who prefer equality to freedom. Such an assumption, however, would badly misconstrue the core values of the socialist, communist, and social democratic traditions. It has often been said that the attitude toward equality represents a fundamental line of demarcation separating the political valences of left and right.[1] Yet we could reach the conclusion that left and right could be mapped on to a stark choice between mutually exclusive ideals of equality and freedom – the left cherishing the former, the right defending the latter – only by ignoring crucial questions about the unique nature of modern social egalitarianism. What, precisely, do social egalitarians hope to equalize? Is equality to be valued for its own sake or for its relationship to some further ends? The answers to questions like these will reveal that for the social egalitarian tradition, equality and freedom, far from being opposed to one another, are instead deeply intertwined.

Equality

The virtually limitless ways in which human beings might be equal or unequal can be grouped into two broad categories. We could – as children begin to do from a very young age – consider the balance of individual capacities or qualities against one another. Some are stronger than others, some more intelligent or skillful, some better looking. Two questions immediately present themselves as we start to think in these terms. First, how should differences in individual capacities or qualities be measured? Should we employ one scale or many? Should we measure strength by the number of push-ups people can execute in a given time period or by the weights they can lift overhead? Should intelligence be measured by the ability to solve mathematical equations and logic problems or by the ability to recognize spatial patterns? Is there an objective test for beauty or is it always in the eye of the beholder? Second, are the differences we register on the various scales innate elements of our individual biological nature, the products of environment, upbringing, cultural adaptation, and opportunity, or some combination of these?

The possibility that individual qualities might be produced or influenced by external factors implies the other way in which equality and inequality might be registered: people may differ in their possession of or access to goods of all kinds. Material resources may jump to mind first, but we should also include in this category legal rights, political rights, and various forms of status, recognition, or respect. Here, too, problems of measurement crop up. Equality or inequality in the distribution of material goods is seemingly the least problematic, although the relative importance of different resources might be questioned. The distribution of legal or political rights may be clear *de jure*, but highly contestable *de facto*. Status, recognition, and respect are virtually impossible to consider except in subjective terms.

For political philosophy, the social distribution of goods is a deep and defining issue. In some cases, political philosophy arrives late on the scene, serving merely to explain and legitimize an existing social distribution of wealth, rights, or respect. At other times, it acts as a precursor, making the case for the virtues of a future redistribution of social goods.[2] But to the extent that different traditions of political philosophy advocate equality, they do so always in one of two ways. Equality can be considered for its own inherent value or, alternatively, for its instrumental value – for its ability to support or promote other values.[3] A related distinction can be drawn between satiable political demands for equality and open-ended, radical egalitarianism. The former category would consist of arguments for equality in the distribution of particular rights or resources, while the latter would suggest a concern with all forms of relative difference in society.[4] Though it may seem obvious that the call for a particular form of equality is not the same as a call for the equalization of all potential forms of difference, a common move by some opponents of social egalitarianism is to obscure this difference, causing all demands for equality to appear absurd.[5]

Debates over the meaning, relevance, and legitimacy of equality stretch back to the origin point of political philosophy itself. We have little evidence of the ways in which the ancient Athenian aristocrats who ruled the city-state prior to the rise of the democracy understood or legitimized their power.[6] What we do know is that as the *demos* – the ordinary people – successfully challenged the power of the hereditary aristocracy during the fifth century BCE, they developed new concepts of equality: *isonomia* (equality before the law), *isotimia* (equal respect), and *isogoria* (equal rights to political speech and action).[7] For the ancient Athenians, of course, these applied only to native-born adult men and strike our contemporary sensibilities as elitist, rather than egalitarian. Yet, as Josiah Ober points out, within the context of ancient Greek history and culture, the exclusion of women, foreigners, and enslaved prisoners of war from legal and political rights is less notable than the fact that under the democracy, a form of legal and political equality had been created among men of different class backgrounds.[8]

It is critical to underscore, in this sense, just how much of an exception Athens was. Democratic uprisings occurred in some other ancient Greek city-states, but no other government resembling the Athenian democracy – with its sovereign assemblies and assignment of public offices by random lot – sustained itself in the ancient world. Closest, perhaps, was the Roman republic, before the rise of the emperors. A popular assembly of adult male citizens was a central element of government, though as compared with its Athenian counterpart, its power was severely restricted. The Athenian assembly was fully empowered to make law by majority vote and votes were counted equally. Roman assemblies could only approve or reject proposals sent to them by the elite members of the Senate and votes were differentially weighted according to property ownership. In his *Republic*, the Roman jurist and political thinker Cicero contends that it is inequality in the distribution of power which leads to good government and a stable society.[9]

Even more radical forms of legal and political inequality were the norm throughout most of the larger civilizations of the ancient world and became the norm in Europe during the feudal era. In the world of European feudalism, political rights were the exclusive property of a narrow aristocratic elite. Different packages of legal rights were assigned on the basis of membership in hereditary caste groups. To be born in a particular place, either as a serf on the commons or as a noble in the manor, was to possess certain corresponding rights and responsibilities: for serfs, an obligation to produce agricultural surpluses for the nobility, and a right to residence and subsistence production on the commons; for nobles, a right to appropriate the economic surplus and a responsibility to respect the residence and subsistence rights of the serfs.

The violation of those rights and responsibilities through acts of enclosure would eventually suggest a new form of legal personhood. Beginning in the sixteenth century, landowning aristocrats began fencing off areas of what had been common land, evicting former serfs, and converting what they now declared to be private property into sheep pastures, hoping to take advantage of the booming wool market. Though it was in no sense a movement for legal equality, the process of enclosure implied the idea that in their economic activities and transactions, human beings were abstractly equal: a landowner's decision to enter the wool trade was no different from a homeless vagabond's search for employment in the city. Both could be seen as making their way in the world using private resources for private gain. Both now had neither social rights to the means of subsistence, nor economic responsibilities to others. Living in a world thoroughly made over in this image, it can be difficult for us to recognize its origin in anything other than raw human nature, as Smith and Locke do. But the economic individual – the owner of private property, existing through transacted exchanges with other, similar owners – was the product of a legal revolution, the result of deliberate political decisions.

This new way of understanding the relationship between the individual and society is reflected in Hobbes's *Leviathan*, one of the first landmark works of social contract theory. Although it appears completely unremarkable when read in the contemporary context, when the book was first published in England in 1651, surely the most striking element of Hobbes's argument would have been his opening presumption of general human equality. While acknowledging the obvious range of differences between individuals in strength or intelligence, Hobbes specifically denies that anyone has been granted by virtue of birth a natural right or ability to rule over others. Equality, for Hobbes, is natural to us. Hierarchy (which Hobbes believes is vital for our survival in stable societies) must be engineered and put into operation through a contractual agreement.[10] On the one hand, Hobbes is a firm believer in the efficiency and efficacy of monarchy.[11] On the other hand, he brushes away the sentimental mysticism surrounding aristocratic power, revealing it to be the result of human, rather than divine, will.

By the eighteenth century, classical liberalism was pushing at the boundaries of the Hobbesian social contract and arguing for what could be seen in many ways as a return to the legal and political standpoint of Roman republicanism.[12] No better example of this can be found than the American revolutionaries' institution of legal and political equality between adult male property owners, deemed to belong to the correct racial category. The American revolution was carried out in Roman costume, complete with separate assemblies for the elite and the masses (the Senate and the House of Representatives), matching neoclassical architecture in the nation's capital, and slaves toiling in the fields.

The progress of the notion of equality in the history of political thought, then, cannot be mapped by a smooth, upward-sloping line. Rather, what emerged with the birth of capitalism was a debate between liberal and social egalitarian concepts of what it meant to be equal. Thus, the first great wave of enclosures in the sixteenth century sparked not simply justifications of the present state of affairs or nostalgic longings for the past, but Thomas More's vision of a radically reordered society in *Utopia* (1516). As the book opens, More's narrator suggests that England's sudden surge of crime can be traced to the conversion of feudal commons into sheep pastures and the eviction of peasants from the land.[13] What follows is a traveler's account of the island nation of Utopia, whose citizens have effectively abolished private property. The Utopians wear identical clothing and have no locks on their doors.[14] On Utopia 'Everyone gets a fair share, so there are never any poor men or beggars. Nobody owns anything, but everyone is rich – for what greater wealth can there be than cheerfulness, peace of mind, and freedom from anxiety?'[15]

The fictional context in which the narrative is set and the deliberate distance placed between author and imagined narrator leave some room for doubt as to More's own position regarding material equality. Fewer questions of this sort surround Gerrard Winstanley and the Diggers, who occupied and cultivated rural waste grounds, building four small communes between 1649 and 1651. Stiff resistance from local landowners quickly ended the Diggers' experiments in communal living. But in his published works, *The New Law of Righteousness* (1649) and *The Law of Freedom* (1652), Winstanley continued to promote the argument that social equality and economic betterment for the working class could be achieved through common ownership of land.[16]

By the early nineteenth century, the takeoff phase of the Industrial Revolution in western Europe and North America had already begun to produce tremendous social disruption, rampant outbreaks of disease, dramatically shortened life expectancies, and general misery for the working classes now crowding tenement houses in the new factory towns.[17] The so-called utopian socialists, Charles Fourier and Robert Owen, reacted to the increasingly disastrous conditions of capitalist industrialization by developing plans for small, intentionally established rural communes. In *The Theory of the Four Movements* (1808), Fourier argued that communal villages (or 'phalanxes') should be established on which residents would live, work, and equally divide the proceeds of their labor.[18] Owen (himself the owner of a textile mill in Scotland) was commissioned in 1817 to produce a report on the causes of urban rioting in Britain. He went well beyond his charge, arguing that the source of the riots lay in the squalid conditions of working-class neighborhoods and creating a detailed blueprint for the complete reorganization of urban settlement.[19]

The general thrust of the utopian socialist reaction to early industrial capitalism can be seen in Edward Bellamy's *Looking Backward*, the nineteenth-century analogue to More's *Utopia*. Bellamy employs a fictional narrator to suggest that American capitalism's combination of tremendous productivity and vast wealth inequality was eventually transformed to produce a future society premised on economic equality.[20] On the one hand, the utopian socialists clearly highlight the instrumental value of equality, arguing that an equal distribution of property will result in social peace and stability. Owen, for example, believed that there would be no need for courts or prisons in his 'Villages of Cooperation' – equality would eliminate the root cause of crime.[21] On the other hand, there is also a claim in the works of the utopian socialists that justice itself demands an even distribution of social resources among all members of the community, suggesting an inherent value to equality.

Justice, however, was precisely what liberal political philosophers argued would be violated by any attempt at producing greater social equality. All individuals, liberal thinkers contended, possessed natural rights to the ownership and use of private property. If wealth was already distributed unequally, creating a society to match the utopian socialist vision would require the use of government's coercive power to confiscate the property of the haves for redistribution to the have-nots. Thus, the redistribution of property would create a skewed distribution of the one good liberals insisted on allocating in equal quantities: freedom.

Freedom

Liberal political thought originated in the rejection of aristocratic privilege and the call for legal equality – at least, in its earliest versions, among property-owning adult men. In this sense, the particular legal regime called for by liberalism suggests a concern not only with equality, but with a type of freedom. Individuals, according to liberal political philosophy, should be equal with one another in their rights to think, speak, and live as they choose.[22] Each of those rights – but particularly the last – implies the use of and benefit from material resources, which for liberals are rightfully owned and most efficiently utilized as pieces of private property.

For liberals, the individual ownership of private property is not an institution requiring political engineering, though it sometimes requires political defense. The individual's ownership of him- or herself is understood as directly connected to the ownership of external resources through which the self is maintained and actualized.[23] The freedom to own and use private property, then, is a natural right, requiring only the absence of coercive forces that might prevent individuals from pursuing their own good in their own way. This is the type of liberty that Isaiah Berlin refers to as negative freedom (the absence of external forces steering or restricting individual choice), which he distinguishes from positive freedom (particular material resources that allow us to engage in particular activities).[24] Milton Friedman illustrates the idea of negative freedom with his suggestion that Robinson Crusoe, trapped on his island, lacks not freedom, but power.[25] So long as no government compels him to obey speed limits or pay his man Friday a minimum wage, he remains free. This, for the liberal, is paradise: the private island on which the law can never be anything more than the individual owner-ruler's whim.

In political terms, providing individuals with negative freedom means, very simply, staying out of their way. It is sometimes said that for liberal political thought, the best form of government is one with limited power, but this is incorrect. The liberal state needs abundant power to protect individual claims to private property from those who might attempt to violate them. A weak government would be unable to deter thieves, uphold valid contracts, or defend against foreign invasions – all of which the liberal society requires. What liberalism truly values is not a government with limited power, but a government whose power occupies a limited scope. Most importantly, government's interference with private property and voluntary economic transactions should be minimized. For the liberal, government is merely a necessary evil, a nightwatchman or an umpire, employed only because people are not saints and cannot always be trusted to respect the rights of others. The greater part of everyday life should proceed through the negotiation and execution of voluntary exchanges. Buyers and sellers will meet one another in the marketplace, where, as Smith puts it, 'every man may purchase whatever part of the produce of other men's talents he has occasion for.'[26]

As such transactions proceed, of course, it becomes increasingly likely that legal equality will come to coexist with material inequality. Some entrepreneurs will succeed in the market, others will fail. Winners will absorb the property of losers. And whether success comes through skill or luck or accident, the winners of market competitions will gain relatively durable advantages that may be used in future contests. Real estate markets offer a prime example. On More's imaginary island of Utopia, because some homes will naturally have better locations than others (more convenient access to services, better views, etc.), houses are allocated by lot and reassigned every ten years.[27] If we were to open a real estate market on Utopia, some houses would quickly become more valuable than others. The owners of these homes (which would now need locks on their doors) would be able to borrow against their value (assuming that we also open a credit market or, at least, grant the Utopians access to the lending departments of offshore banks) and purchase rental properties. Eventually, just as in real market societies, a small class of property owners would have significant and durable economic advantages over a larger class of propertyless tenants.

Yet the emergence or existence of an inequality is – in most cases – not enough to settle the question of its justice or injustice. There may be some who would insist that any uneven distribution of any good is always unjust, but most people (and certainly most political philosophers) would accept that some forms of inequality are perfectly legitimate. Granting physically handicapped persons exclusive rights to parking spaces closest to the doors of shops or offices, for example, creates a type of inequality, but one that most of us would probably accept as just. For political philosophy, the justice or injustice of a form of inequality is usually related to the context in which it exists and the fundamental beliefs we hold about the justice or injustice of relationships, transactions, and situations.

Liberal political thought, for example, holds that voluntary actions undertaken by individuals are just, to the extent that they are not coercive to others.[28] Voluntary transactions between individuals, therefore, would also be just – a point Robert Nozick famously employs as a foundation for his argument that wealth inequality in a market society is in no way unjust. According to Nozick, the results of voluntary transactions between legal equals are nothing more than what individuals have themselves freely chosen. If we can consider it just that legally equal individuals should be allowed to make choices about the use of their powers and resources, then by extension we must consider the outcome of their willing-buyer, willing-seller transactions to be just, as well. As Nozick puts it, 'Whatever arises from a just situation by just steps is itself just.'[29] Thus, if one among us becomes richer than the others by offering for sale a good or service many of the rest of us want, the resulting distribution of wealth may be unequal, but it is not unjust.[30]

Perhaps even more fundamental for liberal political philosophy is the belief that it is human nature to be self-interested. When put into the context of a market environment, however, self-interested individuals may end up unintentionally benefiting one another: 'It is not from the benevolence of the butcher, the brewer, or the baker, that we expect our dinner, but from their regard to their own interest. We address ourselves, not to their humanity but to their self-love, and never talk to them of our own necessities but of their advantages.'[31]

This, of course, is Smith's 'invisible hand' at work: although we go into the market intending to satisfy our own needs and wants, we leave having satisfied the needs and wants of others, as well.[32]

Thus, for liberals, any redistribution of wealth to create greater material equality would be unjust in two ways. First, the provision of particular resources (forms of positive freedom) would come at the cost of a quantity of negative freedom individuals would be forced to surrender. If the one member of our society who has grown rich by offering on the market what the rest of us want is made to turn over a certain quantity of wealth for redistribution, not only would the outcome of voluntary transactions be coercively reversed, the freedom of wealthy individuals to do what they choose with their property would be usurped. Equality, in other words, could be had only through the use of unjust, coercive means, and only at the cost of individual freedom. Second, the usurpation of individual choice (presumably by government) and the pursuit of some uniform collective good, such as equality, would clash with our self-interested, acquisitive nature. Human beings, according to liberalism, can be brought together to pursue collective purposes only accidentally, with the collective good arising spontaneously out of each individual's search for his or her own desires. Any attempt to engineer social outcomes in advance or, worse yet, to depend upon natural feelings of solidarity or benevolence, would be doomed to end in disaster.

It is often assumed that social egalitarian political philosophy is founded on exactly such a belief in a benevolent and solidaristic human nature. In the *Discourse on the Origins of Inequality*, Rousseau unquestionably rejects the Hobbesian view that before the birth of civilization, law, and government, human beings would have existed in a state of perpetual warfare. Sympathy, he argues, is just as natural a sentiment as is self-interested desire.[33] For Rousseau, it is life under the conditions of social inequality which turns us into the murderously self-centered creatures Hobbes imagines us to be by nature.[34] Hasty readings of Rousseau sometimes leave the impression that he therefore believes human nature to be exemplified by the image of the 'noble savage' and that a return to primitive conditions will also return us to a state of peace and harmony. The *Discourse on the Origins of Inequality*, however, offers no such suggestion. When he turns to his proposals for the reform of government in *The Social Contract*, Rousseau does not call for a dismantling of civilization, nor does he presume the perfectibility of human beings. The society Rousseau describes in the latter text will have a highly participatory form of government, but it will have government and law.[35] Rousseau makes clear that material equality will help to create social stability, but he does not suggest that equality alone will create perfect social order.[36]

Within the social egalitarian tradition, the utopians (such as Fourier and Owen) come closest to contending that, given conditions of material equality, the benevolent and solidaristic side of human nature will displace all violent, self-centered urges. In the history of political thought, however, it is really the anarchists who propose that law and government are ultimately unnecessary and that perfect social peace can be had through the spontaneous flowering of human nature itself.[37] In this sense, they have much in common with the liberals, who also believe that unguided individual choices will ultimately result in the best form of social life. The anarchists simply take the argument one step farther, holding that the liberal use of law to defend private property and uphold contractual agreements is still too restrictive and stunting of the development of free and harmonious communities.

The utopian socialists and the anarchists, though, have little in the way of evidence to demonstrate that their understanding of human nature is fundamentally correct. The intentional communities built along utopian socialist or anarchist lines have been few in number, small in size, and brief in duration.[38] More importantly, a materialist interpretation of human nature is forced to contend with the very mixed record of human behavior.[39] In the grand sweep of history and in the minutiae of everyday life, we find generosity next to genocide, and self-sacrifice next to selfishness. A political philosophy built on the expectation that either pure self-interest or pure benevolence characterized human nature would surely be on weak foundations.

Yet a materialist reading of our behavior reveals another aspect to human nature that is far more vital to social egalitarian political philosophy than altruism. Human beings share with other animals a need to transform elements of the natural environment in order to sustain life. Like other animals, we are inescapably connected to the material world – and to physical activity, work, labor in that world – by our need to breathe, eat, drink, and shelter ourselves. But as Marx points out in his *Economic and Philosophical Manuscripts*, our species is unique in its forms of activity that go beyond the satisfaction of basic physical needs:

> It is true that animals also produce. They build nests and dwellings, like the bee, the beaver, the ant, etc. But they produce only their own immediate needs or those of their young; they produce one-sidedly, while man produces universally; they produce only when immediate physical need compels them to do so, while man produces even when he is free from physical need and truly produces only in freedom from such need.[40]

Our unusual cognitive capacity and intense self-consciousness lead us to engage in activities that are radically different from those of other life forms we know of. Artists paint and sculpt, even when no one buys their works. Poets write poems that no one will ever see, much less accept in exchange for food. Weekend players gather for baseball games with no one paying their salaries and having purchased their own equipment. Our Saturday tennis matches, our chess games in the park, our garage band jam sessions contribute nothing to the satisfaction of hunger or thirst. All of them, in fact, come at the cost of time and energy we must spend working in some form of paid employment. Thus the great sense of relief most of us feel when the weekend arrives – not because we will then slip into a state of unconscious hibernation for forty-eight hours, but because after five days of working for someone else to pay the rent and buy the groceries we will finally be able to do what we want to do, to choose our activities freely.

In this respect, social egalitarianism shares a point of agreement with liberalism. Both traditions of political philosophy find something particularly important in the phenomenon of human subjectivity. For liberals, negative freedom is vitally important precisely because individuals differ from one another in their goals, desires, tastes, and preferences. The essence of the individual, then, can only come to life in the spaces that are absent of external coercive forces. To be human, for liberalism, is to be an individual; to be an individual is to be free from powers that would make our choices for us. But what Fourier, Marx, and other social egalitarians point out is that physical necessity is itself a form of power constraining our freedom:

> Simple or physical freedom [...] is the condition of a poor man who has a very small fixed income, only enough to provide the barest necessities, a military ration. He enjoys an active physical freedom because he is not forced to work like the laborer who has no independent income [...] Such a man is, nonetheless, considerably more free than the laborer who is obliged to work lest he die of starvation and who has just one day a week of active physical freedom – Sunday.[41]

> Hence the worker feels himself only when he is not working; when he is working he does not feel himself [...] His labour is therefore not voluntary but forced, it is forced labour [...] Its alien character is clearly demonstrated by the fact that as soon as no physical or other compulsion exists it is shunned like the plague.[42]

That most working people 'work for the weekend' is evidence of the fact that the choices we make when driven by physical necessity are of a different character than those made when food and shelter are not at issue. When it is our free choice to do so, most of us gladly leave our places of paid employment to pursue more satisfying activities.

What is a free choice? While meaningful choices will always be limited by constraints of some type, we can think of free choices as those in which our capacity for deliberation plays an essential role. As actors, we experience this in every waking moment. As observers, however, it is obscured from us. Unable to view consciousness directly, we cannot be certain of the extent to which independent deliberation, coercion, or manipulation is responsible for the choices of others. Thus, we are left with only one way to evaluate the extent to which choices are made freely: we must assess the conditions under which choices are made.[43]

Choices between alternatives have necessary preconditions. First and foremost, deliberation and choice – like all other forms of action – require space. Everything that happens must happen somewhere.[44] Human actions require, at a minimum, the physical necessities that sustain life: air, food, water. Further specification of the types of action we are interested in will impose more particular demands for resources to serve as their necessary preconditions. Material resources, therefore, are the preconditions of meaningful choice. The person who lacks musical training is not free to choose to play an instrument. The musician who possesses ability but no instrument is similarly unfree.[45] To use Isaiah Berlin's terminology, we could say that positive freedom is the precondition of meaningful negative freedom. With respect to my ability to make free choices, a vacant space cleared of coercive forces is meaningless to me unless I also possess material resources with which to actualize my powers, potentials, preferences, and desires.

The point must also be understood in broader, social terms. If material resources represent the preconditions for free choice, the distribution of material resources will determine the distribution of meaningful freedom. 'Necessitous men,' as Franklin Roosevelt put it in his 1944 State of the Union message, 'are not free men.'[46] Tellingly, after denying that material resources have anything at all to do with freedom in his 'Robinson Crusoe' example, Milton Friedman protests that in an authoritarian socialist society, advocates of capitalism would be unfree if they lacked the necessary means with which to press for their cause.[47] It depends, in other words, on whose ox is being gored. From a position of relative privilege and influence, Friedman finds no contradiction between freedom and material deprivation. Imagining a hypothetical situation in which his ready access to the levers of power might be taken away, the connection between positive and negative freedom suddenly becomes clear to him.

The recognition of this connection – between individual freedom and its necessary preconditions – resonates throughout the social egalitarian tradition:

> In place of the old bourgeois society with its classes and class conflicts there will be an association in which the free development of each is the condition for the free development of all.[48]

> Every socialist movement's proud and beautiful goal is a society based on freedom, mutual cooperation, and solidarity, where all exploitation is abolished and each individual's free and harmonious development is the condition of everyone's free development.[49]

> Democratic socialism is an international movement for freedom, social justice and solidarity. Its goal is to achieve a peaceful world where these basic values can be enhanced and where each individual can live a meaningful life with the full development of his or her personality and talents and with the guarantee of human and civil rights in a democratic framework of society.[50]

We can say, in fact, that this idea represents social egalitarianism's most fundamental value. If the pursuit of freely chosen activities is an essential part of human nature, the good society should endeavor to provide its members with real possibilities for the free development of their capacities to the greatest extent possible.

What does it mean, though, to say that in the good society, the free development of each is the condition for the free development of all? Why is it not enough to say, as liberals and anarchists do, that individual freedom is to be valued above all else? The relationship between positive and negative freedom reveals that individual choices and actions are premised on the availability of material resources. The wealthy individual is meaningfully free in ways that the materially deprived individual is not. But as more members of society gain access to necessary resources, the opportunities for free activity and development multiply. This is not the case simply because of the summing up of individual capabilities, but because collaboration with others leads to new possibilities that even the richest of individuals acting alone will never know.

G. A. Cohen offers a particularly insightful interpretation of this idea by analogy. The musicians in a jazz band pursue their individual development and fulfillment in collaboration with others. The extent to which each individual player is able to develop his or her talents is conditioned by the ability of others to do so as well. But this does not mean that individual interests, desires, or capabilities are sacrificed for the pursuit of collective aims. Rather, it is the coming together of individuals able to pursue their development as musicians that creates a collective venue in which that development takes place.[51] Each individual's ability opens avenues of possibility for all the rest.

This, then, is the reason for social egalitarianism's stress not only on freedom, but on equal freedom. It is also the reason why social egalitarian political philosophy concerns itself with the distribution of material resources and, therefore, with the organization of a society's economy – the question to which we turn next.

THREE

Economy and society

There is, of course, a classical liberal or capitalist interpretation of the argument laid out in the previous chapter. If it is important that society offer individuals the chance to develop their capabilities and interests freely, and if material resources are necessary preconditions for such development, why not organize the economic aspects of social life according to the principles of the market? Individuals will acquire the particular resources they need and desire, exchanging freely with one another on a willing-buyer, willing-seller basis. As they do so, their free activity – the free development of their capacities – will spontaneously give rise to social order. As Friedman puts it: 'To the free man, the country is the collection of individuals who compose it, not something over and above them [...] He recognizes no national purpose except as it is the consensus of the purposes for which the citizens severally strive.'[1] For the classical liberal, markets are the exemplary realms in which the free development of each is the condition for the free development of all.

From the individual's perspective, the market is simply a field of opportunity in which to search for the necessary resources with which to pursue subjectively held interests. Viewed from the other side of the lens, though, the market can be seen as a social strategy for economic coordination. As individual buyers and sellers of goods and services pursue their various interests and desires, the answers to an enormous number of economic conundrums appear. How much broccoli to the suburbs of Cleveland this week? How many sixteen-inch tires to Chicago? Allow individual owners of private property to decide for themselves how much of this they are willing to trade for how much of that and the problems solve themselves, quickly and efficiently.

More important for classical liberalism, however, is the claim that markets coordinate the distribution of scarce economic resources without the use of coercion.[2] Under certain circumstances, this is entirely correct. The hypothetical model of market distribution in which prisoners of war reallocate their Red Cross packages provides the classic example. Each package contains the same goods (chocolate, cigarettes, powdered milk, etc.), yet each soldier's preferences are different: one smokes, another does not, one is allergic to chocolate, and so on. Establishing a market in which items could be traded freely would allow each soldier to end up with the mix of goods he prefers, while simultaneously respecting each one's freedom to pursue his interests as he sees fit.

The best case that can be made for classical liberalism's understanding of freedom rests here, in the vision of individuals free to pursue their own good in their own way through the trading of resources on an open market. Yet the happy outcome of the 'Red Cross package' example is not due to the pure dynamics of market exchange alone, but to the conditions under which the individual transactors enter the market. In this case, they do so under conditions of material equality. Each soldier begins with an equal distribution of resources and, as a result, it is subjective desire alone which determines the reallocation of goods: cigarettes will go to smokers, chocolate to chocolate lovers. But if the initial endowments with which individuals enter the market vary, we can no longer be certain that the allocation of goods by a market mechanism will match up with subjective preferences. If the ticket to a basketball game costs more than I am able to spend, my love of the game alone will not get me in the door. With more money at my disposal, I may be able to buy basketball tickets simply as a novelty, despite the fact that I do not care very much about the game at all. If my income is large enough, I could purchase an entire season's worth of front-row seats simply to have them available in case, on a whim, I decided to take in a game. As I do so, the market price of basketball tickets rises, putting them farther out of the reach of those with smaller incomes than my own.

Further problems arise if we consider more closely the particular nature of the resources individuals will need in order to pursue their interests through market transactions. In addition to sufficient quantities of a fungible means of exchange (most conveniently, money), market participants require information about the range of available goods and their prevailing prices. In order to make sense of this information, they will need to be literate, numerate, and have at least a basic understanding of the institutions that make up their society. Yet there is no independent market incentive to provide universal education.[3] Entrepreneurs may be willing to open private schools for those who can pay what the market will bear, but if we assume any significant inequality in wealth or income, we must also accept the possibility that the price of basic goods such as education may rise beyond the point at which all members of society will be able to afford them. One form of inequality may then spiral into another. Unequal incomes may lead to an uneven distribution of educational resources and information, leading to advantages and disadvantages in market bargaining, leading to wider income and wealth gaps. These, in turn, result in inequality in the chances for individual freedom.

But there is also a deeper threat to freedom that arises from the use of markets as tools for economic coordination. Markets for luxury items – gold watches, diamond earrings – exist because wealthy individuals possess effective demand for such things: desire combined with an ability to pay the prevailing price. Labor markets, however, exist for a different reason. Economics textbooks typically suggest that a labor market reflects the existence of differing preferences: some choose to work in exchange for valuable resources, others prefer free time and leisure. Real markets, though, are not abstractions floating somewhere beyond the world in which hunger, thirst, and cold will eventually mean the end of life. Once the basic resources necessary for maintaining life are controlled by a wealthy elite, the rest will be left with no option for survival other than to offer for sale their own ability to do work.

> When can I go into the supermarket and buy what I
> need with my good looks?[4]

Until then, those who lack the land and capital necessary to earn a living independently must enter the labor market.

Coercion – precisely what classical liberalism promised would be avoided through the use of markets – now reenters the picture, though it takes on a unique appearance: 'Oppression by force was replaced by corruption; the sword, as the first social lever, by gold.'[5] Having entered the labor market, workers will find that their bargaining power differs considerably from that of their employers. Taken together, the conditions under which labor markets arise and the balance of bargaining power within them create a situation in which workers are exploited by those who own the means of production.

Exploitation

In its most basic sense, exploitation refers to the taking of unfair advantage.[6] Liberals and social egalitarians would surely agree that this is involved in both feudalism and slavery. Slave owners and feudal lords benefit disproportionately from the labor of slaves or serfs who are compelled by law to participate in the relationship. Capitalist wage labor, however, presents a more intriguing, more difficult, and more controversial scenario. Here, the law steps back and washes its hands of the question of economic responsibility. In a market economy, no one is legally obligated to work for anyone else. As a result, for liberal political thinkers, exploitation is eliminated. 'The employee,' Friedman explains, 'is protected from coercion by the employer because of other employers for whom he can work.'[7] Because the exchange of labor for wages is voluntary, it may appear unequal, but it is in no way unfair.

Liberal economists would add a second line of defense to the charge that capitalist wage labor is exploitative: the exchange of labor for wages on the market is fair not only because it is voluntary, but because it represents an equal exchange. This is so, according to orthodox liberal economics, owing to the marginalist theory of value. All goods, according to the theory, are subject to declining marginal utility. My first cup of coffee in the morning is worth more to me than my second, which is worth more to me than my third, and so on. Put into the context of a market environment, the marginalist theory of value tells us that goods are worth whatever people will pay for them. Value is identical with market price. Thus, the worker who sells forty hours of labor power for $300 receives exactly what his or her labor power is worth. The fact that workers are not forced to work for particular employers ensures that they will sell their labor power to the highest bidder. The fact that employers are not forced to hire particular employees ensures that they will pay no more than what an additional worker's labor power is worth to them. It is of no significance, then, to the liberal economist that factory workers, CEOs, and majority shareholders in large corporations receive different incomes. According to the marginalist theory of value, all parties in the marketplace receive exactly what their efforts are worth.

But while orthodox liberal economics excels at explaining the appearance of market prices for various goods, it has always struggled to explain the item of chief importance to every business owner: profit. Capitalist firms purchase raw materials, tools, machines, and labor power. Wage workers, under the direction of managers, assemble finished products or supply services to customers. At the end of the day, the costs of production are deducted from the firm's gross sales receipts and whatever remains is claimed by the owners of the firm as profit. If this were only an occasional happy accident, it might require no explanation at all. Full-scale capitalist economies, however, rely on the regular generation of positive profits – a fact entitling social scientists to enquire as to their source.

What causes the value of a finished good or service to exceed the value of the goods that went into producing it? Some say that market conditions alone are responsible for positive profits. Market prices depend on consumer demand, so the successful entrepreneur buys low and sells high. To test this hypothesis, imagine an economic system composed of two actors on a small island who control two different goods. *A* owns a stock of ten umbrellas; *B* owns a stock of ten volleyballs:

A (10U)
B (10V)

The total amount of value in the system is:

10U + 10V

In the springtime, it is equally likely that on any given day it might be sunny or raining. Umbrellas and volleyballs are equally desirable and exchange one-to-one. In the summer, the value of volleyballs goes up: one volleyball is now worth five umbrellas. *A* wants a volleyball and negotiates an exchange with *B*:

A (5U, 1V)
B (5U, 9V)

B appears to have profited by taking advantage of market conditions – selling high – yet the total amount of value in the system remains unchanged:

(5U, 1V) + (5U, 9V) = 10U + 10V

Thus, if exchange alone were the source of profit, one firm's profits would always have to be paid for by another's losses – a condition that cannot and does not occur in a real economy. 'The capitalist class of a given country, taken as a whole,' Marx suggests, 'cannot defraud itself.'[8]

Similar problems crop up in the abstinence theory of profit, a favorite of liberal economists. According to the abstinence theory, profits result because business owners are rewarded for investing their resources, rather than consuming them. Abstinence, though, may justify capitalists' claims to profit, but it fails to explain their appearance. As economist James Devine points out, professional poker players take risks and abstain from consuming their investment capital during games, but their winnings represent only the redistribution of resources from one set of hands to another. Abstinence does not create new value.[9]

It was Marx's contention in his works on political economy that the labor process added new value to existing materials and released stored value from tools and machines. Yet if the value of a finished good was equal to the value of its components, no profit would be created and no capitalist would remain in business. Thus, Marx argued in *Capital*, the successful operation of an ongoing capitalist economy requires that workers continue to add value to the goods they produce past the point at which their own wages have been paid for. Profit (or in Marx's terminology, surplus value) is positive only if workers receive back in wages less than the full value of their contribution to production.[10]

The central problem that has always dogged Marx's explanation of the source of profit hinges on the distinction between value and price. If profits result because workers contribute more value to goods during production than they receive back in wages, it should be possible to convert market prices into labor values. Economists have argued for years, however, that no mathematical formula can be found that will consistently and accurately perform the transformation.[11] If market prices ultimately result from the willingness of buyers to trade one good for another (as the marginalist theory holds), the labor used to create a product might have no definite quantitative relationship to its selling price and, therefore, no definite relationship to a firm's profit margin.

It is clear, however, that the labor process adds value to objects in the world. As economist Duncan Foley suggests, this dynamic becomes easier to see if we move from the micro-level viewpoint of the individual firm to the macro-level view of a large-scale economy. From this perspective, a widely accepted measure of economic output – net domestic product – represents the money value added to an economy over time by labor.[12] With respect to the question of exploitation, we could now ask whether workers' wages are equal to the value added to the economy by the labor process. Foley estimates that in 2005, each hour of labor added an average of $50 worth of value to the US economy.[13] In the same year, average hourly wages for US workers stood at $16.13.[14] Further, if the marginalist theory of value were sufficient to explain the division of business revenue between wages and profit, wages should rise along with productivity. Yet countries with similar levels of productivity (for example, the USA and Germany) have very different average wages.[15]

A full examination of the complex and highly technical debate among economists over theories of value would go well beyond the scope of this book. On the one hand, it is clear that a simplistic labor theory of value will fail to tell us anything useful about the question of exploitation in contemporary economic relationships. Unless it is possible to translate market prices into corresponding labor values, we cannot gauge the distance – if any – between what an individual worker is paid and what he or she contributes through labor to the finished product. On the other hand, if the labor theory of value is treated not as a tool for explaining individual market prices, but for questioning the distribution of income within an economy, it opens useful insights unexplored by marginalist economics.

Consider, for example, the division of economic surpluses in the context of different legal regimes. Over the course of a year, the labor of serfs on a feudal estate creates new value in the form of agricultural produce. How is this new value divided between the direct producers and the owners of the means of production? The nature of feudal law means that there is no ambiguity in the distribution of income between classes: surplus produce beyond the immediate subsistence needs of serfs is the property of the nobility. If we now transform feudalism into capitalism, introduce legal equality and a labor market, the precise nature of the division of newly produced value between classes is suddenly obscured. Of the new value produced by workers in a capitalist society, what portion is profit, to be claimed by the owners of the means of production, and what portion is to be paid as wages to the direct producers? If aggregate profits are positive, aggregate wages must be less than the amount of new value added to the economy by the labor process. The labor theory of value, then, poses a question as to the equality of the wage labor transaction at the systemic level. In any functioning capitalist economy, the working class as a whole receives back in wages less than it contributes to the expansion of net domestic product.

We must recall at this point, however, that the purportedly equal value of labor power and wages was only one response offered by liberals to the claim that capitalism involves the exploitation of workers.

The primary defense of capitalism against charges of exploitation has always rested on the voluntary nature of market transactions. Imagine, for example, that in our two-commodity model economy, A and B once again negotiate an exchange of goods. As before, we will endow A with ten umbrellas and B with ten volleyballs. Climate change has caused the island to be pounded with rain on most days and as storm clouds loom on the horizon, B negotiates with A for an umbrella:

A (9U, 5V)
B (1U, 5V)

The circumstances under which the transaction takes place give one party an advantage over the other: the resources controlled by A are more valuable than those controlled by B. According to a marginalist theory of value, though, the exchange is equal and fair: B wants an umbrella and is willing to give up five volleyballs in order to get one. A possesses an advantage, but by the standards of liberal economists it is not an unfair advantage. As long as both parties are the legitimate owners of their respective goods and neither is coerced into accepting the terms of an exchange, the fact that one party possesses resources of greater value than another does not make a transaction between them exploitative.

Is there any point at which the possession of an advantage begins to compromise the voluntary nature of an exchange? Hobbes famously maintains that even actions performed out of fear are engaged in freely.[16] When a gun is pointed at my head and I am asked to choose between my money and my life, I can still accept a bullet rather than surrender my wallet. Most of us, though, would recognize some degree of difference between the voluntary nature of a choice between two different restaurants at which to have dinner this evening and a choice between eating or starving to death. In the case of our model island economy, the nature of A's advantage (fair or unfair) and B's choice (voluntary or coerced) may become clear only if we know how badly B needs protection from the rain.

The classical liberal argument that transactions in the labor market are voluntary is rooted in the fundamental liberal claim that individuals possess natural rights to self-ownership and to the ownership and use of private property. Locke, for example, holds that a chain of property relationships connects the right of self-ownership with corresponding rights to material resources acquired through the use of labor power:

Thus the Grass my Horse has bit; the Turfs my Servant has cut; and the Ore I have digg'd in any place where I have a right to them in common with others, become my Property, without the assignation or consent of any body. The labour that was mine, removing them out of that common state they were in, hath fixed my Property in them.[17]

We should note here the modification of Locke's labor theory of property by the laws of contract. The turfs cut by Locke's servant have not been mixed with Locke's labor, yet he stakes a claim to them, implying that the servant's labor power is, in effect, an extension of his own. This is, in essence, the classical liberal justification of the employer's right to a firm's profits. Workers may directly mix their labor with raw materials to create finished goods, but they do so under contract – their labor power has already been sold to the employer in exchange for a wage. Assuming that Locke's servant is a wage laborer and not a slave or a serf, his sale of labor power is voluntary because, as a legally free and equal individual, he is under no obligation to provide labor to anyone. In the same way, Locke is under no obligation to put his turf-cutter into operation, through his servant's labor or anyone else's. He is perfectly free to allow it to sit idle in the tool shed.

Liberal political thought, then, sees property as abstractly identical. The property right that I have in my body and its powers is, for the Lockean liberal, identical to the property right that a group of stockholders have in a multibillion-dollar factory. Just as I may choose to work or to loaf, the factory owners may choose to put their plant into operation or to leave it idle. Just as I have a right to benefit from the use of my labor power, the factory owners have a right to benefit from the use of their facilities. But here, we reach a critical point about which social egalitarian and liberal political philosophy disagree. For social egalitarians, property cannot be considered as a monolithic abstraction. Instead, productive property must be distinguished from personal property.

At first glance, the line of demarcation between these two categories might appear to be drawn by physical characteristics – perhaps size, mass, or value of resources. Farms and factories represent significantly larger concentrations of resources than do shirts or shoes. Yet between the extremes is a considerable gray area. I can use my car only on weekends to drive myself to and from the beach, where

I like to swim. Alternatively, I can hire someone to drive it as a taxi and collect the net proceeds as my profit. Without altering its physical characteristics, my car is transformed from a piece of personal property into a piece of productive capital. The real difference, then, between personal and productive property lies not in the physical characteristics of objects, but in the ways they are used. That said, it is also clearly the case that some objects will make better pieces of productive property than others. My chances of success in opening a café would be significantly greater with a prime retail storefront, several commercial espresso machines, pastry cases, refrigerators, etc., than if I were to set up my coffee-maker on a cardboard box outside my apartment building.

The image of the sidewalk lemonade stand is often used to teach the basics of orthodox liberal economics to schoolchildren: an entrepreneur specializes in the production of a particular good, bringing together raw materials, creating a finished commodity, and trading with others who similarly specialize. Thus, as Smith proposes in *Wealth of Nations*, the market economy is supposedly born.[18] What is missing from this image, however, is the central characteristic of capitalism: the wage labor relationship. The imaginary lemonade stand economy contains no wage laborers because productive property remains evenly distributed. Every economically active member possesses sufficient resources to survive as an independent, productive entrepreneur. A skewed distribution of productive resources would lead to a very different set of economic and social relationships, but one more closely resembling the real world of capitalism. For social egalitarians, the meaningful difference between personal and productive property is to be found here. An uneven distribution of personal property may reflect differences in subjective preferences (guitarists will own guitars, pianists will own pianos), but will not necessarily alter the ways in which the members of a society make their living. An unequal distribution of productive property, however, will create conditions under which those who lack sufficient resources with which to produce and exchange commodities will be forced to choose between wage labor and starvation.

The first political economist to recognize the effect this situation would have on labor market bargaining was in fact not Marx, but Smith, who pointed out that employers were fewer in number than wage laborers (making it easier for them to organize among themselves) and that the possession of a significant stock of productive property would allow a business owner to survive without workers much longer than workers could survive without employment.[19] Given conditions of legal equality, some workers might become business owners themselves, although this path is nowhere near as open as classical liberals typically suggest it is. The amount of capital required to start up a business in most industries is high, the amount of credit available to those with limited collateral is typically low, and the majority of new businesses do not survive for more than a few years.[20] More importantly, in a capitalist economy, the profitability of firms depends upon the availability of workers whose wage demands do not exceed the profit margin. A small number of workers may be able to transform themselves into capitalists, but in order for them to succeed, a much larger number must remain behind, continuing to work for wages.[21] Legally free workers may be able to refuse to work for a particular employer, but the vast majority must work for some employer.

Hobbes may be correct that a choice made under the threat of death is still a free choice in the strictest sense, but most contemporary legal systems refuse to honor agreements negotiated at gunpoint. In the legal context, contracts involving an absence of meaningful choice or a significant inequality in bargaining power are declared to be unconscionable and are unenforceable.[22] On similar grounds, social egalitarians argue that capitalism involves an unfair advantage rooted in the inequality in bargaining power between employers and employees. It is not necessary, in other words, to calculate microeconomic labor values for individual products or services in order to define capitalist exploitation. At the macroeconomic level, the expansion of net domestic product reveals the creation of new value by labor. The division of that new value between wages and profit reveals the advantage held by employers: their ability to negotiate labor market contracts on terms favorable to themselves.[23] The magnitude of the advantage held by employers is represented by the differential between productivity and wage gains.[24] The unfairness of the employers' advantage lies in the fact that, for workers, entry into the labor market is voluntary only in the very limited sense of being a choice between life and death.

Eliminating the causes of exploitation

If capitalist exploitation is rooted in the employer's ownership of the means of production and appropriation of the commodities that workers produce, one possible strategy for the elimination of exploitation immediately presents itself: workers should either be recognized as the owners of the goods they produce or be fully compensated for their value. Yet this simple and direct approach to addressing capitalist exploitation encounters both philosophical and practical difficulties. Philosophically, the idea that individuals have legitimate claims to the goods they directly produce clashes with the social egalitarian principle that the powers and abilities of the individual are always intertwined with the powers and abilities of others in society.[25] Practically, a highly developed society could not function if each individual received and consumed precisely what he or she produced. Even if it were possible to determine the value of individual labor contributions to finished goods, deductions would still need to be made to pay for reinvestment in continued production, research and development, administration, and the provision of public goods.[26]

Thus, rather than direct individual appropriation by workers of their products, the most important social egalitarian strategy for eliminating the causes of exploitation has been collective ownership of the means of production. In the *Communist Manifesto*, for example, Marx and Engels argue for the centralization of credit through a national bank, public control of transportation infrastructure, and the expansion of nationalized enterprises.[27] But while the *Manifesto* situates the assumption of public control over the means of production in the context of a revolutionary seizure of power, many in the social egalitarian tradition have held that industrial capitalism's own trajectory of development would bring it near enough to this transformation that the jump from private to public ownership would not be such a long one. Bellamy's imagined future America is one in which the progression from capitalist to collective ownership has been a process of gradual evolution:

> The movement toward the conduct of business by larger and larger aggregations of capital, the tendency toward monopolies, which had been so desperately and vainly resisted, was recognized at last, in its true significance, as a process which only needed to complete its logical evolution to open a golden future to humanity [...] a monopoly in the profits and economies of which all citizens shared.[28]

Public ownership of industry had been made technically feasible, Engels argued, by the separation of ownership and management in the modern corporation.[29] If companies were already owned by shareholders who played no immediate role in day-to-day operations, nothing other than political opposition stood in the way of turning all citizens collectively into the owners of the means of production.

One version of this strategy can be seen in the Swedish Social Democratic Party's wage-earner funds. Originally conceived in the 1970s by Rudolf Meidner, the plan required privately owned companies with more than fifty employees to issue new shares of stock each year, equal to 20 percent of the firm's profits. The new shares would be held by wage-earner funds, controlled by trade unions and government. As they grew in value, the funds would pay for social expenditures. As they grew in proportion to privately held capital, the funds would be able to exert leverage over corporate policy. The plan was put into effect in 1983, but fierce opposition from business interests forced the wage-earner funds to be diluted and eventually dissolved.[30]

As the outlines of the Meidner plan suggest, the question of the ownership of economic resources is always connected to the question of their control. For those social egalitarians who advocate collective ownership of the means of production, centralized economic planning and direction has usually been a significant part of their overall vision. Even the relatively simple pre-industrial economy imagined in More's *Utopia* utilizes a system of planning for the allocation of agricultural labor.[31] But during the twentieth century, as successful revolutions made collective ownership of the means of production a reality in several industrializing states, economic planning necessarily became more elaborate and intensified. Three elements of the centrally planned economies in the Soviet Union, China, and Cuba indicate their break from the workings of capitalist markets. First, economic priorities were set by government leaders, rather than by business owners acting in response to private interests or market indicators. Second, enterprise plans were coordinated in the context of a long-term strategy, rather than being allowed to clash with one another in the anarchy of market competition. Third, social or patriotic motivation was intended to replace the profit motive as an incentive to economic success.[32]

At least two aspects of centralized economic planning can be seen to correspond with the aims of social egalitarianism. First, to the extent that governments stand as representatives of citizens, collective ownership and central planning mean that workers own and benefit from the means of production. Second, economic planning and regulation can be used to deal with the crisis-ridden nature of market capitalism – a phenomenon identified by Marx and Engels in the *Communist Manifesto*:

> Society is suddenly thrust into a condition of temporary barbarism; a famine, a general war of annihilation appears to have cut off all means of life; industry and commerce appear to be destroyed, and why? Because there is too much civilization, too many goods, too much industry, too much commerce.[33]

Economic crises occur in agrarian societies because of the sudden loss of productive capacity: drought, flooding, pests, or disease. But during the recessions that regularly strike capitalist economies, unemployed workers are left standing outside fully functional factories and shops filled with goods. Recessions or depressions occur in capitalist economies not because of a loss of productive capacity, but because of the anarchy of markets: uncoordinated investment decisions sometimes produce optimal economic outcomes and sometimes lead to mass unemployment. The politically coordinated targeting of investment may not always produce success, but it can at the very least be aimed at the achievement of specific goals. The outcomes reached by the market are always unforeseen accidents.

It must be added, though, that because modern history's prime examples of centralized economic planning were created by revolutionary governments in relatively underdeveloped countries, the main goal aimed at by economic planning was industrialization. The nineteenth-century social egalitarians had assumed that their political objectives would be pursued in the context of advanced industrial development and relative economic abundance.[34] The basic steps toward industrialization, however, clashed in fundamental ways with the goals of social egalitarianism. Industrialization, regardless of the region or era in which it occurred, required tremendous sacrifice, claimed millions of lives, and paid dividends to ordinary working people only decades after its first stages had been completed. To the extent that parties, movements, or governments inspired by social egalitarian political philosophy used the tools of economic planning to achieve industrialization, they typically did so at the cost of properly social egalitarian aims.

Economic planning itself is value neutral and might be directed toward any number of political ends. Hitler's genocidal attempt at conquering Europe was launched using the tools of central economic planning, but it was also stopped by them. Not only Stalin's government, but also Roosevelt's used centralized industrial planning and resource allocation to win World War II. The first problem, then, for collective ownership and central planning as specifically social egalitarian strategies has to do with the connection between the political preferences of citizens and the power of government planners. Even assuming a strong popular majority in favor of social egalitarian goals, what assurance can citizens have that government officials entrusted with tremendous power over the allocation of economic resources will make decisions genuinely reflective of those aims?

Liberal political philosophers have long maintained that, as compared to the potentially tyrannical power of centralized economic planners, markets represent a model of economic democracy: individual consumers 'vote' for their preferences, the aggregation of which ultimately leads to the allocation of resources. As we have seen, though, unless wealth and income are equally distributed, some economic preferences will receive more consideration than others. To the extent that markets can be thought of as elections for the allocation of economic goods, material inequality will mean that some voters are able to cast multiple ballots.[35]

Social egalitarians in favor of collective ownership and central planning have argued that genuinely democratic elections could be used to hold government planners accountable to citizens.[36] On the one hand, some of the questions that might be posed regarding the effectiveness of such a model could be asked of any form of electoral democracy: Will citizens take the time to educate themselves about the issues and to participate in the process? Will elected officials pursue the common good or will they cynically seek only to maintain their own power? On the other hand, some vitally important questions about the feasibility of democratically controlled central planning are specific to the economic realm: Can elections be held frequently enough to communicate citizens' economic preferences to government officials? To what extent can citizens cope with the vast range of possibilities for the prioritization of economic resources?

The problem of information volume alone constantly bedeviled the Soviet Union's centrally planned economy. One of the key virtues of market mechanisms is their ability to manage an astoundingly large number of interrelated resource allocation decisions by radically decentralizing the decision-making process. Reducing the number of decision-makers from millions of consumers to a handful of government officials allows for significantly greater control over economic outcomes if all goes well, but simultaneously increases the possibility of crippling shortages in the event of an oversight.

The replacement of market mechanisms by planned allocation also raises questions about incentives and productivity. In short, if economic allocation is detached from the profit motive, why should workers work and entrepreneurs innovate? The problem of incentives for workers appears only if employment and income are detached from labor contributions. But More's Utopians and Bellamy's future Americans, just like twentieth-century Soviet citizens, continued to live under a social obligation to exchange work for income.[37] Entrepreneurship and technological innovation would seem to present greater difficulties for collective ownership and central planning, although here, too, both the fictional imaginings of egalitarian societies and the real-world examples of planned economies suggest some possibilities beyond the profit motive. Bellamy, for example, proposes that a sense of patriotic duty would lead citizens to contribute their best efforts.[38] And while the twentieth-century Soviet economy was unquestionably less dynamic and innovative than the capitalist economies of the West, it cannot be said that it lacked technological innovation altogether. Soviet scientists won Nobel Prizes in the fields of physics and chemistry and succeeded in launching the first satellite into orbit. Scientists, engineers, and inventors (much like artists and scholars) are often motivated by nothing more than a deep fascination with their field of work, its problems, and its possibilities.

The incredible dynamism of industrial capitalist economies, though, leaves no question about the fact that the profit motive can be highly effective at driving technological innovation. During the twentieth century, the furious rate at which new products and productive techniques were developed by privately owned firms vastly outstripped the comparative abilities of state-owned enterprises in the centrally planned economies. Profit-driven innovation, of course, will tend to gravitate toward the sectors of an economy with the greatest profit potential. Plastic surgery techniques, for example, have advanced far more quickly than has the development of high-quality, low-cost housing. Basic scientific research, which typically has no immediate connection to the production of saleable commodities, would be virtually impossible to conduct without support from non-market means.

In other words, collective ownership of the means of production and centralized economic planning face considerable operational difficulties, but they are by no means technically impossible. Thus, the real question for social egalitarian political philosophy is not so much the feasibility of collectivization and planning, but their usefulness in pursuing particular objectives. In a very simplistic sense, it could be argued that collective ownership of the means of production would eliminate exploitation by definition. By making each member of society a joint owner of the means of production, the power of a capitalist class to win favorable terms in labor market bargaining would vanish. Yet employees and employer would continue to confront one another under a system of public ownership.[39] The practical realities of government management of economic resources mean that corruption could threaten to turn government into an exploiter. Without effective means of holding government officials accountable to citizens, political managers may begin to think and act in ways indistinguishable from those of private owners.

Even more importantly, though, the elimination of exploitation in a narrow technical sense may fail to address the key concerns of social egalitarianism. Marx, for example, makes the case that with the simple collectivization of property,

> the community is simply a community of labour and equality of wages, which are paid out by the communal capital, the community as universal capitalist. Both sides of the relation are raised to an imaginary universality [...] The first positive abolition of private property – crude communism – is therefore only a manifestation of the vileness of private property trying to establish itself as the positive community.[40]

Exploitation, it must be remembered, is a concern for social egalitarians not simply because it involves coercion or unfairness, but because it leads to a maldistribution of the chances for human freedom. To say that the separation of ownership from management in the modern corporation makes collective ownership of the means of production technically possible is also to say that a change in ownership may not change the ways in which people live and work. Transforming the community into a universal capitalist may do nothing to support the free development of human capacities. Marx's critique of crude communism, then, suggests that collective ownership of the means of production cannot be an end-goal for social egalitarianism, but simply one possible strategy through which its goals might be achieved.

Yet the distinction between means and ends has at times been lost as political philosophers concentrated their attention on optimally configured visions of a reformed society. The conflation of aims with final end-states is most conspicuous in the utopian socialist tradition. More, Bellamy, Owen, and Fourier present to us complete pictures of social life in which underlying political values are nearly indistinguishable from the institutions or practices that have been used to attain them. Revolutionary enthusiasm, though, was also capable of shifting the focus of political thought from ends to means – strategic objectives being easier to fix with clarity and precision than concepts of justice or freedom.

From the late nineteenth century to the last quarter of the twentieth, the call for a reversal of this agenda was attributed to 'revisionists' or 'reformists' within the social egalitarian tradition. In Germany, Eduard Bernstein declared, 'To me, that which is generally called the ultimate aim of socialism is nothing, but the movement is everything.'[41] The British Labour Party politician Anthony Crosland reiterated that socialism was not 'a particular social structure,' but 'a set of values, or aspirations, which socialists wish to see embodied in the organization of society.'[42] Revolutionary leaders, though, often adopted a very similar outlook. In his assessment of the transition from capitalism to socialism, Engels stressed that a proper approach to the question would be one recognizing not unrelated metaphysical states of being, but dialectically connected processes of change.[43] Lenin's New Economic Policy, introduced to the Soviet Union in 1921, created a hybrid economy with both private and public sectors, effectively acknowledging that socialist goals could be pursued using a mixture of market and non-market tools.[44]

For his part, Milton Friedman has argued that such hybridity is impossible. The choice between markets and planning as tools for social organization, Friedman maintains, is a rigidly binary one.[45] In reality, of course, economic planning and the operation of markets are never mutually exclusive options. At the microeconomic level, every capitalist enterprise begins the production process with planning.[46] At the macroeconomic level, every existing industrial economy encompasses market mechanisms, publicly owned enterprises, and government regulation of economic activity. Contrary to Friedman's contention, the impossibilities lie not in the middle, but at the extremes. As much as the poor performance of the Soviet economy pointed out the severe limitations of centralized economic planning, the fatally turbulent nature of unrestricted laissez-faire capitalism was demonstrated conclusively by the Great Depression. The return to market fundamentalism in the USA and the UK during the 1980s and 1990s led directly to the Great Recession of 2007–10.

But if the choice between economic means – private and public, markets and planning – is not strictly exclusive, the focus of political thought must shift back to the question of aims and values. Collective ownership of productive property has at times been put forward by social egalitarians as a strategy for the elimination of exploitation. Its possibilities of success, however, are limited in two ways. First, collective ownership of the means of production may fail to eliminate exploitation in absolute terms because society cannot guarantee that each member will receive back in income or benefits the precise value of the labor he or she contributes. Second, any lack of effective oversight may allow public managers to take advantage of their positions, becoming de facto owners and exploiters. The transfer of ownership from private to public hands is a means, not an end in itself. Unless other elements of social and economic life are transformed, collectivization of productive property will fail to address social egalitarianism's concern with the distribution of freedom.

Modifying the effects of exploitation

In practice, social egalitarian parties, movements, and policies have never concentrated exclusively on eliminating the causes of exploitation, but have also looked to ways in which to modify its effects. Economic exploitation is rooted in class control of the means of production. One of the ways, therefore, in which the effects of exploitation might be dampened is through the counterbalancing of class power.

It is easy enough to construct a hypothetical in which the balance of class forces Smith perceived in the world of laissez-faire capitalism would be reversed. Imagine a capitalist economy in which all workers are members of one highly effective, thoroughly cohesive labor union.[47] Strikes are legal, no worker will cross a picket line under any circumstances, and the right to strike is protected by government. The size and cohesion of our one big union has allowed it to amass a tremendous endowment of cash to be used as a strike fund. Local rights to private property are respected, but investment flight is prevented by strictly enforced laws prohibiting the movement of capital to foreign countries. Under such conditions, the bargaining power of workers would meet or exceed that of employers.

The basic elements of this hypothetical highlight the foundations of class power in a capitalist economy and the ways in which it might be more equally balanced. First and foremost, where productive property is privately owned, the balancing of class forces requires the existence of a strong state capable of effectively regulating economic activity within its borders. The full range of government regulation of the economy, therefore, contributes to the balancing of class forces and the dampening of exploitation:

> The concentration of economic power in few private hands must be replaced by a different order in which each person is entitled – as citizen, consumer or wage-earner – to influence the direction and distribution of production, the shaping of the means of production, and the conditions of working life. This will come about by involvement of the citizen in economic policies, by guaranteeing wage-earners an influence in their workplace, by fostering open and accountable competition both domestically and internationally and by strengthening the position of consumers relative to producers.[48]

Product safety specifications, professional licensing requirements, banking and finance regulations all transfer power over economic resources from private to public hands, allowing citizens to make collective decisions about the ways in which property can and cannot be used in society.

Class power is also equalized through the political support of collective bargaining and labor union rights. The employer's structural advantage in labor market bargaining can be at least partially overcome by legalizing strikes and prohibiting the hiring of replacement workers during a labor dispute. Historically, socialist, communist, and social democratic parties both in and out of government have led the movements for workers' rights to organize and to bargain collectively with their employers.

The power of organized labor, however, is always undercut by the threat of unemployment. Thus, one of the most effective means by which social egalitarian policy-makers have sought to balance the distribution of class power is the pursuit of full employment. In an economy in which significant portions of productive property are privately owned, public investment in labor-intensive sectors can be used to absorb unemployment and strengthen the bargaining position of workers. The fact that full employment will have the effect of raising workers' wages is directly connected to the core values of social egalitarianism. As Donald Sassoon notes, 'Any increase in unemployment, particularly when coupled with a reduction of social protection, is tantamount to an effective decrease in personal freedom.'[49] Material resources form the foundation for meaningfully free choice – positive freedom is the precondition of negative freedom. The full weight of this point becomes clear in the context of the social egalitarian view of human nature. If human beings are self-conscious makers of subjective meaning, the ability of a society to provide all of its members with equal chances for freedom is a fundamental criterion of its commitment to justice – giving people what they are due.

The social distribution of wealth, therefore, is not only an issue with respect to the control of productive property. Access to resources of all kinds matters to social egalitarians because of their commitment to the ideal of equal freedom. On these grounds, some within the tradition advocate strict material equality. The utopian socialist designs, for example, are premised on an equal distribution of resources to all of a community's members. George Bernard Shaw argued for a similar policy of rigorous income equality to be applied to the modern industrial society as a whole.[50] The objection has often been raised that equal distribution would sap productivity by eliminating material incentives to labor. On the one hand, the examples of successful egalitarian communes (such as the Israeli kibbutzim) suggest that a sense of duty or moral responsibility can act as an incentive to work. On the other hand, the ethics of the kibbutz require a level of social transparency only possible in a very small community.[51]

A more powerful objection to the pursuit of strict income equality has been put forward by Amartya Sen, who points out that because of the natural differences between individuals in strength, innate skill, and disposition, equal incomes would in fact result in the provision of different degrees of benefit.[52] A necessary distinction arises here between equality's inherent and instrumental values. If material equality is valued for its own sake, spartan homogeneity would serve not only adequately, but efficiently. This, in many ways, is More's vision in *Utopia*: a pre-industrial world in which a radical form of material equality is made possible by strict cultural limits on behavior, consumption, and subjectivity. Critics have often projected this image forward, attributing it to modern conceptions of social egalitarianism, but this is incorrect. From the Industrial Revolution onward, social egalitarians argued not for a leveling down of material wellbeing, but for 'equality of the highest standards.'[53] Modern social egalitarianism, in other words, is concerned with the instrumental value of material equality. The distribution of resources matters because it directly affects the real capacities and possibilities people will enjoy in their lives.

Sen's point, however, is that the equalization of capacity is likely to require some differences in material distribution, rather than absolute sameness. Marx makes a similar argument in his critique of the German Social Democratic Party's 1875 platform:

> But one person is physically or mentally superior to another, and hence contributes more work in the same time or can work longer [...] Furthermore: one worker is married, another not; one has more children than another, etc., etc. Given equal productivity and hence an equal share in the socialized resources for consumption, one worker will in fact receive more than another, be richer than another. To avoid all these faults, rights would have to be unequal, instead of equal.[54]

The principle that should ultimately guide material distribution in the good society, Marx suggests, is one of the most famous social egalitarian slogans: From each according to their ability, to each according to their needs.[55] What is meant to be equalized, according to this principle, is not the distribution of resources, but the distribution of opportunities for self-realization.[56]

Of course, the search for all possible human capabilities and the matching of resources necessary to equalize their distribution across a large population would quickly exhaust the productive capacity of even the most highly developed society. A more realistically achievable strategy might be based on the equalization of a limited set of core capabilities by ensuring equal distribution of goods for which all members of society share common needs.[57] This approach to material equality will never satisfy the radical liberal or libertarian. The provision of any good across a community as a whole requires the collection and redistribution of resources: taxation and public spending. And who is to say, the liberal will ask, that the portion of my income you intend to seize in order to pay for universal public education is not better spent on my own consumption of fine cigars?

From the libertarian point of view, all goods are ultimately subjective. To rank some as more socially valuable than others is simply to grant preference to a particular individual's tastes.

What we might identify as core capacities, however, have important foundational and compounding effects that alter their equation with other goods. The capacity for life itself is the basis of all human action. Thus, physical necessities – food, clean water, shelter, sanitation, and a sustainable environment – function not simply as goods, but as the preconditions for our enjoyment of any good. Healthcare and education act in even more dynamic ways as multipliers, expanding the range of choices we might make and goods we might pursue. Transportation and communication infrastructures similarly extend our abilities to engage in a wide variety of self-chosen activities. Insurance and pension funds help to defend our capacities for free activity against common misfortunes and the predictable process of aging. The provision, in other words, of certain forms of positive freedom – those connected to core human capacities – may cost us a quantity of negative freedom at the outset, but repay the investment in kind, many times over.

All of these goods can be supplied by private entrepreneurs as market commodities. But in this form, the goods necessary for supporting and extending core human capacities will be supplied unevenly in terms of both quantity and quality. Goods from which potential consumers can be easily excluded will be supplied by markets, but only at prices that will rule out equal distribution. Given an open market, for example, education will be offered for sale as a commodity. Its high cost, however, will mean that only the very wealthy will be able to afford it. Universal education can be supplied only as a decommodified public good: openly available to all and paid for by the mandatory pooling of community resources.

Goods from which individual consumers cannot be excluded will not be supplied at all by private entrepreneurs because of the problem of free-riding.[58] The defense of a sustainable environment, for example, cannot be adequately parceled into marketable commodities. Although a handful of environmentally conscious consumers may be willing to pay for reforestation or carbon exchange, the vast majority will enjoy the benefits of such action without contributing to the costs. Even Friedman, an advocate of market capitalism in nearly all circumstances, admits that goods such as law enforcement and national defense would be impossible to supply if individual consumers were allowed to choose how much or how little they would like to purchase.[59]

Yet while the problem of market failure – the inability of markets to provide certain goods – can be readily demonstrated both theoretically and historically, the study of economics alone cannot settle the question of what, if anything, our response to it should be. Questions of this order can be answered only by political philosophy. Thus, as much as public goods may appear at times so ordinary as to be unworthy of serious consideration, they are in fact connected to contentious political debates and pivotal forms of social power. All but the most radical anarchists will admit the need for certain resources to be decommodified. Social egalitarians, however, have always made the supply of public goods – and the expansion of such supply – central to their political agenda:

> A democratic society must compensate for the defects of even the most responsible market systems. Government must not function simply as the repair shop for the damage brought about by market inadequacies or the uncontrolled application of new technologies. Rather the State must regulate the market in the interests of the people and obtain for all workers the benefits of technology, both in work experience and through the growth of leisure time and meaningful possibilities for individual development.[60]

For the broad social egalitarian tradition, the supply of public goods is a vital keystone because of the unique possibilities public goods hold for equalizing the distribution of meaningful freedom.

For More's Utopians, who have eliminated private property entirely, all goods are essentially public. More's careful focus on certain goods, though, suggests their particular importance to his overall vision. Utopian children are cared for in public nurseries before attending public primary schools. Later in life, adults continue their educations by means of public lectures. Healthcare is supplied universally, as is the most basic good of all: food. Utopians are free to take food home from community groceries and cook for themselves, but most prefer to take their meals at public dining halls.[61]

Bellamy, too, imagines a world in which food has been decommodified. Like the Utopians, his future Bostonians eat at least one of their daily meals at public restaurants. Public space emerges in Bellamy's vision as a means of equalizing the distribution of comfort and beauty. 'Nowadays,' the narrator's host, Dr Leete, says, 'there is no destination of the surplus wealth so popular as the adornment of the city, which all enjoy in equal degree.' A pre-electronic system of public broadcasting connects corps of musicians acoustically to homes throughout the city.[62]

A similarly extensive vision of the supply of public goods appears in an intriguing modern analogue to the utopian imagination, *Novye Elementy Rasseleniia* (New Elements of Settlement), published in the West as *The Ideal Communist City*.[63] The book was produced in the late 1950s by a team of Moscow University academics led by architect Alexei Gutnov. The bold socialist utopianism driving the book's vision seems to run counter to our typical expectations of Soviet scholarship. But we sometimes forget that the late 1950s was a time of relative intellectual openness and socialist renewal in the USSR, initiated by Khrushchev's 1956 condemnation of Stalin's tyranny. It was in the climate of the Khrushchev Thaw that Gutnov and his colleagues set about to create what architectural critic James Mayo called 'a concrete spatial agenda for Marxism.'[64] Mayo's description of the book is meant to indicate something beyond the use of architecture simply to legitimize political authority. Rather, in *The Ideal Communist City* we find an attempt by socialist architects and planners to 'interpret physically what their political ideals could achieve.'[65]

Public space immediately comes to the fore in the basic principles around which Gutnov and his colleagues organize their design for the urban community of the near future:

1 Equal mobility for all. Residential sectors are at equal walking distance from the center and from the forests and parks surrounding them.

2 Distances are planned on a pedestrian scale. No home is so remote from the center or from the park area that it cannot be reached by a reasonably short walk.

3 Elimination of danger from vehicular traffic. Rapid public transportation operates outside the pedestrian area yet is linked centrally with the New Units of Settlement. (Its circuits carry people from home to work and from home to home.)

4 Green belts. Every sector is surrounded on at least two sides by open land.[66]

The planners' central concern with social equality is immediately apparent in their preference for pedestrian and public transportation over privately owned vehicles, as well as in the related bias toward high-density apartment housing. Here, they clearly acknowledge what is at stake in the planning of residential developments:

> Ideal conditions for rest and privacy are offered by the individual house situated in the midst of nature. But this is an expensive kind of well-being [...] The villa is the traditional retreat of the leisured minority at the top of the bourgeois society. The attempt to make the villa available to the average consumer means building a mass of little houses, each on a tiny piece of land [...] The mass construction of individual houses, however, destroys the basic character of this type of residence.[67]

In their rejection of the American model of suburban sprawl, Gutnov's team specifically notes its unfeasibility in a society premised on equality.[68]

We might assume that in the context of a centrally planned economy, it would be axiomatic for public goods to be the primary focus of any architectural design or urban plan, but this would be to conflate ends and means. Urban planning for the fascist state would command public resources under centralized direction, but might deploy them in the creation of spaces from which the general public was excluded: military facilities or palaces for the officer-elite. The emphasis in Gutnov's vision is not on the question of public or private ownership of economic resources per se, but on the ways in which public goods might equalize the distribution of private freedoms:

> Life structured by freely chosen relationships represents the fullest, most well-rounded aspects of each human personality. These are developed through choices made during the time free from work, on the basis of interests, desires, and cultural options open to all [...] Leisure activity creates numerous individual and material needs. These mean that areas must be assigned to leisure activity, areas that, of course, should be fully accessible to everyone.[69]

The Soviet planners specifically contrasted their vision of public parks, recreational facilities, and club venues with the typical form taken by space devoted to leisure activity in capitalist countries: the shopping center.[70] Yet, rather than assuming that publicly provided forms of positive freedom would satisfy in and of themselves the full range of human needs, Gutnov et al. echoed the social egalitarian understanding of positive freedom as the foundation from which individually chosen paths might be pursued. As contrasted with the liberal version of the good society, however, the provision of positive freedoms in the form of public goods is meant to ensure that the ability to develop individual tastes, preferences, and capacities is not monopolized by a wealthy elite.

As contrasted with what was imagined by the utopian designers, the supply of public goods in the hybrid economies of western Europe and North America was limited. Yet, from the late 1800s to the middle 1970s, social egalitarian parties and movements made considerable progress in developing forms of public insurance and public infrastructure. In 1900, only a handful of European states devoted as much as 3 percent of GNP to social welfare. By the 1960s, social spending in most European countries and the USA had grown to between 10 and 20 percent of GNP.[71] While the first public social insurance system was created in Germany in the 1880s by Bismarck's government – staunch opponents of the growing socialist movement – the introduction of health insurance and a pension plan was meant to undercut the socialists' strength by adopting elements of their agenda. Not long afterwards, the Parti Ouvrier Français, the first French political party to link itself to Marx's intellectual lineage, won election to several municipal governments and began to develop public libraries, a school lunch program, and a small pension plan.[72] By the last half of the twentieth century, the most extensive versions of European social democracy offered citizens comprehensive, universal health and retirement insurance, income security, and a wide array of public sector services.[73]

The progress of social equality during this period could also be seen in the leveling of income distribution. In the USA, the share of national income claimed by the richest 0.1 percent of the population fell from nearly 10 percent in 1915 to 2 percent in 1973. Similar trajectories could be seen for income distribution in the UK and the western European states.[74] This change was neither accidental nor inexplicable. As forms of publicly provided insurance and income support became more robust, workers (particularly in the sectors of the labor market organized by trade unions) gained bargaining leverage. As the bargaining power of workers grew, incomes became more evenly distributed. By the middle 1960s, there was a distinct plausibility to T. H. Marshall's thesis that the highly developed countries were gradually proceeding through a three-stage accumulation of rights: legal rights in the eighteenth century, political rights in the nineteenth, and social rights in the twentieth.[75]

But in the late 1970s, a coalition of organized business elites and their political allies launched a powerful counter-attack against the ideological foundations of third-generation rights. In the UK, Margaret Thatcher led the attack on public goods and the restoration of market principles. In the USA, while Ronald Reagan came to symbolize the assault on 'big government,' the first shots were in fact fired by Jimmy Carter, who announced that a program of 'pain and discipline' would have to be endured in order to reduce the level of government spending.[76] Popular wisdom was gripped by a mania for budget cutting, the most public symbol of which was the deficit clock mounted on a building in midtown Manhattan by a wealthy real estate developer, silently whirring away, recording the trillions in principle and interest owed by the government – a stark materialization of ideology in which state spending loomed overhead like a time-bomb, threatening to explode when the clock ran out. It was often claimed that cutbacks in government spending were made inescapably necessary by the economic stagnation of the 1970s. Yet, in the USA, the ratio of government spending to GDP rose three times faster during the boom years of the 1950s and 1960s than during the recessionary 1970s and 1980s.[77] As Ronald Reagan's first budget director, David Stockman, once revealed, deficit hysteria provided political cover for severe cuts in the supply of public goods, but was never the reason for them.[78]

The foundations of anti-government ideology had been put in place during the early years of the Cold War, with Orwell's *Nineteen Eighty-Four* providing the key literary imagery. For decades, American schoolchildren knew well from exactly which direction the threat to their liberty would come. Let loose the tight leash on government and Big Brother would soon be staring down at us from every wall. Thus, in mounting an advertising campaign in opposition to President Clinton's proposal for a national healthcare plan in 1993, an insurance industry association focused its attack on the image of bureaucracy. The famous 'Harry and Louise' ads featured a middle-class couple discussing the Clinton health plan, gradually revealing its totalitarian implications:

LOUISE: 'This plan forces us to buy our insurance through those new mandatory government health alliances.'
HARRY: 'Run by tens of thousands of new bureaucrats.'
LOUISE: 'Another billion-dollar bureaucracy.'[79]

A firestorm of criticism in the popular media charged that a system of public health insurance would mean the rationing of healthcare. Of course, the vast majority of those in the USA who had access to health insurance were already subject to market-based rationing of care by insurance companies and private Health Maintenance Organizations.

All scarce resources must be rationed in one way or another. Market commodities are rationed based on the ability and willingness of consumers to spend their incomes. Public goods are rationed based on the availability of resources and the political choices made by citizens and their representatives in government. Unlike market-based rationing, however, the supply of resources as public goods allows for the possibility of equality in distribution and access. This is important at times and not at others. Not even the most radical egalitarian would deny that tremendously valuable forms of social complexity and individual subjectivity are fostered by allowing for certain differences in distribution and access. Highly developed economies cannot function and at the same time guarantee that everyone will have simultaneous access to every possible good, service, or tool, just as a jazz band cannot play if every musician has simultaneous access to every instrument. Yet the possibility of any form of meaningfully equal freedom always requires the distribution of resources in the form of public goods.

It is important to recognize that this axiom holds with respect to any and all public goods and not only to a particular configuration of them within some overall social design. Something as simple and ordinary as a public park ensures that the opportunity to stroll or sit in a quiet, beautiful setting is not rationed according to one's income. Something far more complex, such as a system of public healthcare, may enhance the equal freedom the park provides: healthy people are better able than sick ones to enjoy the opportunities a park has to offer. But the possibilities offered by a holistic combination of public goods should not deflect us from noting that each one works in the same basic way to support the capacities for activity, development, and expression that make us free. If meaningful choices can only be made when relevant resources are available, the provision of resources in the form of public goods acts to support equality in the freedom to choose.

Material resources, however, are necessary but not sufficient for freedom to be realizable. In order to create the possibility for genuine freedom, one additional resource is needed: free time. This point was of central importance for Fourier and Marx. Both highlight a distinction between the work that is necessary in order to sustain the conditions of our existence and the activities we are able to engage in when the demands of physical necessity have been met.[80] Each sphere of human activity draws upon the same limited pool of time. Genuinely free activity, then, requires the basic goods needed to sustain life, whatever particular resources are called for by the activity we choose to engage in, and time that is not already devoted to securing the first two material preconditions. For freedom to be possible, time must remain in the day, unabsorbed by the range of necessary activities in the workplace and the household. Thus, in *Capital*, Marx argues that the fundamental premise for an expansion of human freedom is a shortening of the working day.[81]

In one sense, this may mean that under conditions of freedom we would make different choices than the ones we make when forced to concern ourselves with paying the rent and buying the groceries. If I learn that I have been left a large inheritance – enough to live on comfortably for the rest of my life – I may suddenly find that my paid employment no longer holds any appeal for me. Yet it is not so much the nature of the activity itself but the conditions under which I choose it which matter with respect to the issue of freedom. The motions made by the arms and legs of a person struggling to stay afloat after falling from a boat in the middle of a lake may resemble those of a person enjoying a free afternoon by swimming laps in a pool, but they are of a radically different character. I may choose to continue working at my job after learning of my inheritance or cashing in my winning lottery ticket, but the choice that I make is now free in a way that it was not before.

In More's pre-industrial socialist vision, free time is made available by ensuring that all members of the community contribute their labor to necessary work and by restricting the production of luxury goods. The Utopians view pleasure as the goal of life and therefore value free time highly, yet theirs is an earthy, contemplative idea of enjoyment.[82] They work six hours a day, with the remainder 'free to do what they like – not to waste their time in idleness or self-indulgence, but to make good use of it in some congenial activity.'[83]

By contrast, modern social egalitarians will develop different understandings both of what free time might be good for and how it might be made available. In Fourier, Marx, Bellamy, and the twentieth-century political philosophers who follow in their intellectual lineage, the value of freedom is to be found in the expansion of human subjectivity, rather than in its restriction. Marx's early writings are particularly powerful in their call for an emancipation of human senses and capabilities. Quite unlike More's conservative Utopians, Marx sees material and temporal freedom as the opposite of self-denial:

> The less you eat, drink, buy books, go to the theatre, go dancing, go drinking, think, love, theorize, sing, paint, fence, etc., the more you save and the greater will become that treasure which neither moths nor maggots can consume – your capital. The less you are, the less you give expression to your life, the more you have, the greater is your alienated life and the more you store up of your estranged life.[84]

There is a sense here of the new possibilities opened up by transformations More could never have foreseen. By the middle of the nineteenth century, a monastic limitation of life's potential will not be the only way to achieve material wellbeing and an expansion of free time.

We often think of technological innovations as resulting in the introduction of labor-saving devices. Saved labor, of course, should mean saved time. Yet, prior to the Industrial Revolution, a thirteenth-century British peasant worked approximately 1,620 hours per year. After the introduction of a vast range of labor-saving technology, a nineteenth-century British worker put in approximately 3,588 hours per year. In 2005, the average American holding a nonagricultural job worked 2,033 hours per year.[85] Industrial capitalism, as G. A. Cohen points out, seems to result in the confounding combination of more leisure goods with less leisure time.[86]

The improvement of technology tends to lead to increases in productivity: the quantity of goods that can be created with a given amount of labor time. The workers who are able to stitch ten shirts a day using nothing but needles and thread are likely to multiply their output several times over using sewing machines. Once such an improvement in productive technology has been achieved, however, there are three competing possibilities for utilizing its benefits. One option would be for the employer to redistribute saved labor in the form of higher wages. Provided that markets can be found in which to sell the finished goods, more output will mean more revenue, which could be directed back to workers in their pay checks. Alternatively, the newly enhanced flow of revenue could be labeled as profit and sent into the accounts of the employer. But the improvement of technology also holds out the possibility of redistributing saved labor as free time. As productivity increases, the working hours needed to reproduce our standard of living decrease. Assuming that productivity gains are not captured by increases in wages or profits, they remain available as time.

The Industrial Revolution's combination of labor-saving technology with increased working hours, then, is no mystery. The bulk of productivity gains from improvements in mechanical efficiency were redistributed to the owners of privately held factories, mines, and farms in the form of profit. The increases in wages and decreases in working hours eventually won by industrial workers in the highly developed countries were the result of organizing and struggle led by labor unions and social egalitarian political parties. The achievement of the eight-hour working day, now taken to be a standard in the developed world, came only through a protracted and sometimes violent political struggle, not through the wisdom or benevolence of employers or through the wonders of technological improvement alone.

During the twentieth century, the importance of reducing the length of the working day tended to be lost in the underdeveloped countries as parties coming to power under ostensibly social egalitarian banners took up the task of industrialization. The brutality of the period of Soviet industrialization, for example, while inextricably linked to the personality of Joseph Stalin himself and to the immediate demands imposed by the Nazi invasion, also resembles in many ways the brutality of the Industrial Revolution in Britain, western Europe, and North America. The fact that the latter process was driven by the invisible hands of market forces should not obscure the fact that, as a direct result of the push for rapid industrialization, working hours increased dramatically, living and working conditions deteriorated, and the lives of most ordinary working people were cut tragically short.

It should be clear to contemporary social egalitarians, however, just as it was to their nineteenth-century predecessors, that reducing the length of the working day – the redistribution of productivity gains in the form of free time – is a vital keystone to the provision and expansion of equal freedom. For social egalitarian political philosophy, the freedom to sell oneself piecemeal to an employer or to starve is a pitiful version of freedom indeed. The continual improvement of technology can allow us to do better than this, but the decisions arrived at by markets will never lead in this direction. The distribution of free time to all – not just to the wealthy – requires the power of political intervention.

Classical liberals or libertarians will charge that political intervention in the play of markets is itself an unacceptable compromise of individual freedom. But in considering the nature of this debate, it is important to reflect on the fact that all social life requires some restriction of individual choice. Prohibiting some forms of action can result in a net gain of freedom for all. Prohibiting murder meaningfully limits the range of choices available to potential murderers, but also grants a type of freedom to all in society who might now be able to walk the streets with less fear.[87] Thus, if some forms of individual freedom are always lost when we live in society, rather than in isolation, political philosophy should concern itself with assessing relative gains and losses of freedom. For social egalitarians, the provision and expansion of freedom for all is well worth the cost of denying business owners the right to do whatever they choose with their productive property.

The community of equals

Social egalitarian political thought is often assumed to center on the creation of community. Yet here too we can recognize a critical difference between the type of pre-modern conservative communitarianism depicted in More's *Utopia* and the modern interpretation of an egalitarian society.

Just as More imagines his Utopians to have created the possibility of a reduced workday through rigid self-denial, he portrays the Utopian community as one premised on social surveillance and restriction. Utopians are allowed to travel only when in possession of internal passports, watch one another continuously for signs of shirking, and strictly prohibit sex outside of marriage.[88]

This version of the community of equals has often been put forward as the purported ideal of social egalitarian political thought: Equality is possible, but only in the monastery, the kibbutz, or the barracks – the world, therefore, must be reshaped in their image. It is no surprise that this interpretation has most often been insisted on by the opponents of social equality. There are some for whom a cloistered, spartan community represents social perfection, but their numbers are small. If the only way in which meaningful equality can be created is through the radical repression of behavior – identical clothing, constant surveillance, military discipline – the social egalitarian project will have little appeal.

What has too often been ignored is the radical break with More's pre-modern communitarianism announced by the modern social egalitarians. Marx, for example, writes not of a community in which rigidly disciplined behavior results in a leveled-down form of pseudoperfection, but of a world in which the creation of genuine equality would allow for the pursuit of genuinely human relationships. Such a world, he suggests, would not guarantee happiness, only that love would be exchanged for love, and trust for trust.[89] Bellamy echoes his thought, proposing that the creation of a society of genuine equals will free individuals to choose their relationships with one another based on mutual desire and compatibility. 'Wealth and rank no longer divert attention from personal qualities.'[90]

In its modern form, social egalitarianism concerns itself with the expansion of equal freedom, not with the creation of a crude version of equality through the radical restriction of freedom. As the Swedish socialist leader, Ernst Wigforss, once put it, the objective of equality is not identity, but fraternity.[91] Trust and unity come more easily between equals. This is a point (as Rousseau reminded us) that is worth highlighting when considering not only social and economic but also political affairs – the subject we turn our attention to next.

FOUR
Democracy

Most schools of political philosophy accept as a basic premise that for large, heavily populated, highly developed societies, institutions of government are not optional – they are mandatory if reasonable levels of social peace and economic productivity are to be maintained. Within the mainstream of the social egalitarian tradition, formal institutions of government are more important still: they are vitally necessary for counterbalancing the potentially exploitative power of private property and providing the material foundations for equal freedom in the form of public goods.

Yet within the anarchist tradition we encounter the argument that the key goal sought by social egalitarians – maximization of equal freedom for all – can be achieved not by utilizing formal institutions of government, but by abolishing them. It is true that in the history of political thought there are some influential advocates of individual freedom who are wholly unconcerned with freedom's universal availability. Ayn Rand, for example, suggests a vision of human existence in which what matters most is the emergence of great individuals, unrestrained by law or morality.[1] From this perspective, government is nothing more than a tool of the jealous and the weak, used to hobble the truly virtuous. Its elimination would be desirable not because it would offer the possibility of free development to ordinary members of society, but because it would remove an impediment preventing the rise of a genuine elite. The majority of anarchist thinkers, however, hold that their ultimate aims are identical to those of other social egalitarians; that 'every anarchist is a socialist, but every socialist is not necessarily an anarchist.'[2]

The anarchist critique of the state, then, presents two challenges to the previous chapter's argument that government intervention in the economic realm is necessary for the promotion of equal freedom. First, we must assess the claim that social egalitarianism is hindered rather than advanced by the existence of formal institutions of government. Second, to the extent that the anarchist critique of the state is directed against hierarchical arrangements of power in society, it points us toward further questions about the relationship between social egalitarianism and democracy. At its root, democratic theory suggests the rightfulness of political equality. But the precise nature of that form of equality and its nexus with equality and inequality in the economic realm are highly contested territory. Virtually all contemporary political thinkers may claim to be democrats, but the distinctions between their understandings of democracy can make all the difference in the world.

State power

Evidence of state power is easy enough to come by in the stuff of ordinary life. Walking down a public sidewalk, one passes a mailbox, a public school, traffic signs, a police car. Stopping at a café, sales tax is added to the bill. Next to the cash register, a certificate indicates that the health inspector has given the kitchen a passing grade. But from the perspective of political philosophy (which, like other schools of philosophical inquiry, is often concerned with careful examinations of the seemingly obvious and mundane), what does the existence of the state – formal institutions of government ruling over a defined population within a demarcated territory – mean?

Thomas Hobbes's *Leviathan* stands as a landmark in the history of political thought because it is one of the first modern texts to treat the existence of the state as a question, rather than as an assumption. His famous thought experiment in which government is erased from social life ends with the conclusion that, freed of the restrictions of law, society would degenerate into a war of all against all.[3] The crucial links leading from statelessness to chaos are scarcity and property. Without government to define and enforce property rights, all human beings would have natural rights to whatever helped sustain or improve their lives. The scarcity of such goods, however, would set natural rights on a collision course with one another. The right to everything, Hobbes argues, quickly becomes a right to nothing. The purpose of government, then, is to create social peace by protecting formal property rights with a type of coercive force no individual will be capable of resisting.[4]

At times, Hobbes's thought experiment threatens to take on the appearance of a historical narrative. His references to a 'natural condition' begin to settle into a timeline whose next demarcation point is the social contract giving birth to the state. Hobbes's explanation of

government's purpose, however, does not necessarily reveal its historical origins. The fact that the United States government restrains some
forms of conflict over scarce resources on the islands of Hawaii does
not tell us that it arose there specifically in order to do so. Government may have arisen for any number of reasons and may prevent
social conflict only as a side effect of its intended purpose. Yet, even
if we cannot accept Hobbes's thought experiment as an explanation
of history, its structure and direction reveal something interesting
and important. *Leviathan* is a meticulously crafted argument that
seeks to persuade us of the rightfulness of government's existence
and authority. Writing in the wake of the Thirty Years War between
European Protestants and Catholics, and the more immediate context
of the English Civil War, Hobbes is well aware that governments can
and do fall apart. The purpose of his work is not to retell government's history, but to convince us that we should respect and obey
its decisions.

What *Leviathan* reveals to us, then, is the contested terrain of
political obligation. In this sense, we can recognize the text as one
meant to fill the gap left by the weakening of claims to political
authority through divine right after the fragmentation of European
Christianity. Hobbes clearly fears that in the wake of the Protestant
Reformation, religious belief will not be a sufficient foundation for
the legitimate authority of the state. Although certainly a believing
Christian, he sets out to find secular justification for our submission
to law. We owe allegiance to the state, he argues, because its existence
helps to preserve our own.

For Hobbes, any government is better than no government, and
stronger government is always better than weaker government. Hobbes
is a confirmed monarchist who worries that readers of ancient Greek
and Roman political thought will come away with dangerous ideas
about democracy.[5] But here we encounter an intriguing tension in his
argument. Hobbes is certainly no Jefferson, claiming that government
obtains its right to rule from the consent of the governed. Yet he
clearly recognizes the power of consent – that the strength of the state
is ultimately grounded in a popular respect for the law. The difference,
for Hobbes, between monarchy and democracy is not the presence or
the importance of the people's consent to authority, but the proximity
of their consent to policy. In the democratic model, each action taken
by government is potentially subject to the judgment of citizens. In
the Hobbesian monarchy, the consent of subjects is necessary in order

for government to exist, but the act of consenting to government's rule implies a willingness in advance to accept its decisions.

We could say, then, that for Hobbes political obligation is founded on utility. We owe an obligation to the state (and should therefore grant it our consent) because we receive significant benefits from it. The state provides us with a form of security – basic social order and rules regarding property – that we could not obtain as individuals. More contemporary versions of political obligation emerging from democratic theory will propose that our duty to obey the law arises from our participation in the political process. The citizen who accepts the right to a role in shaping the rules of social order is presumed to accept a corresponding responsibility to respect those rules.

Anarchists, however, would be quick to point out that all such considerations of political obligation conveniently ignore a single decisive element: the state and its laws are backed by coercive force. When someone approaches me on a darkened street, brandishes a gun, and demands my money, the transaction that takes place depends upon an imbalance of power. If a particularly clumsy thief happens to drop his gun into a storm drain while attempting to rob me, I feel no continued obligation to pay him. By contrast, when the Internal Revenue Service informs me that I owe tax payments to the government, its claim is voiced in tones of authority, duty, and responsibility.[6] Behind the claim to authority, though, is the state's armed power and the threat of harm if I fail to comply. For the anarchist tradition, this use of coercive force is unacceptable and deeply contradictory with the values of freedom and equality.

Society without the state

The ancient Greek designations of regime type that have carried over into the English language refer to the possession of sovereign power. In a democracy, the ordinary working people (the *demos*) possess the power to rule (*kratos*). Under aristocracy, sovereign power is the possession of the *aristos* – the best, the elite. The absence of government – the condition in which no one possessed the power to rule – would be for the ancient Greeks *anarchia*. But it is the nineteenth-century author and political activist Pierre-Joseph Proudhon who first begins to use the term 'anarchist' to refer to either a movement or a school of political philosophy.

For anarchists like Proudhon, the social egalitarian goal of equal freedom for all is a perfectly admirable one, but its achievement is blocked by the existence of formal government. Equality, anarchists maintain, is impossible in the presence of state power. As Hobbes so powerfully demonstrated in *Leviathan*, it is precisely the radical form of inequality created by the imbalance of power between the state and its subjects which allows for the effective enforcement of law. To be governed by state power, Proudhon charged,

> is to be watched over, inspected, spied on, directed, legislated, regimented, closed in, indoctrinated, preached at, controlled, assessed, evaluated, censored, commanded; all by creatures that have neither the right, nor wisdom, nor virtue [...] Government means to be subjected to tribute, trained, ransomed, exploited, monopolized, extorted, pressured, mystified, robbed; all in the name of public utility and the general good.[7]

Thus, not only are we radically unequal under the power of the state, from the perspective of anarchist political thought we are also radically unfree.

It is often the case that debates between those who have substantial basis for agreement run hotter than disputes between those who share little common ground. The exchanges among anarchists, socialists, communists, and social democrats have at times been particularly sharp not because of the extreme distance between their positions, but because of the relative proximity of their ultimate values. Like the mainstream of the social egalitarian tradition, nineteenth-century anarchists were deeply critical of the power of private property. Like Marx, Proudhon held that the monopolization of productive property by capitalists led to the exploitation of workers and the proliferation of social inequality. The two differed fiercely, however, over how this situation was to be corrected. Proudhon contended that, in an egalitarian society, workers would retain individual rights to the value they produced, measured in labor time. Marx replied in a scathing critique of Proudhon's work that this form of exchange already occurred daily in the capitalist labor market. Progress toward a genuinely egalitarian condition, he argued, would be made not by upholding individual rights to labor contributions, but by developing social rights to necessary goods.[8]

Evidence of similar struggles over the proper approach to shared values can be found in the work of other anarchist thinkers. Property, Emma Goldman wrote, was 'an abnormal institution' recognizing only 'its own gluttonous appetite for greater wealth, because wealth means power; the power to subdue, to crush, to exploit, the power to enslave, to outrage, to degrade.'[9] But what underwrote the power of property was the state.[10] Here, she echoes the logic of fellow anarchist Mikhail Bakunin: if the existence of property depends upon state power and the coercive enforcement of law, the only way to eliminate the domination and exploitation of private property is to do away with the state.[11]

The anarchist critique of state power, however, runs deeper than its attack on the foundations of private property. For anarchist political thought, the maintenance of formal institutions of government leads to an erosion of individual autonomy and responsibility that fundamentally jeopardizes human freedom. The special capacities that give rise to the possibility of freedom, Robert Paul Wolff suggests, are free will and reason. To the extent that we can not only choose but reason about our choices, we become responsible for our actions. This is the basis of moral philosophy. Moral, autonomous, responsible human beings, therefore, cannot obey commands. They must instead engage in independent deliberation and choice. Yet the forfeit of autonomy, Wolff argues, is precisely what is called for in politics.[12]

The anarchist rejection of law, then, is rooted in its powerful advocacy of individual responsibility. For Goldman, the acceptance of such responsibility is nothing short of a crucial step in the history of human development:

> Anarchism urges man to think, to investigate, to analyze every proposition [...] Break your mental fetters, says Anarchism to man, for not until you think and judge for yourself will you get rid of the domination of darkness, the greatest obstacle to all progress.[13]

Thus, for anarchists, individual responsibility is pitted directly against political obligation. To the extent that we are responsible for our own choices, Wolff maintains, we must deny that the state has any authority over us. We can choose to obey the law because it is rational, reasonable, or ethical to do so, but not simply because it is the law.[14] Even more importantly for anarchist political thought, we cannot be coerced to obey the law and remain free.

This does not mean, however, that anarchists propose the dissolution of society. Rather, they argue that the best form of society will be organized through principles of voluntary association. For some anarchist political philosophers, the basis for such a society will be provided by natural dynamics of empathy and cooperation. Countering the Darwinian image of biological evolution as a competitive process, Peter Kropotkin argued in *Mutual Aid* that successful species survived through the emergence of cooperative relationships.[15] Society, Bakunin held, was natural to human existence and in no way contradicted the ideal of individual freedom.[16] The good society, however, would be one consisting of 'voluntary productive and distributive associations' organized 'first into a commune, then a federation of communes into regions, of regions into nations, and of nations into an international fraternal association.'[17]

Anarchism has at times sparked powerful sentiments, particularly within western European and North American youth culture. This is undoubtedly due to the strongly optimistic cast of anarchist political thought and its promise of absolute individual freedom. But anarchist optimism regarding the flowering of cooperative voluntary associations in the absence of state power has little in the way of historical precedent for support and requires assumptions that strain the bounds of credibility.

How, for example, would the anarchist community protect a sphere of individual freedom from physical intrusions by others? Some anarchists hold that violent crimes such as assault or murder would naturally disappear in the stateless society. Crime, Goldman argued, was simply human energy misdirected by political and economic institutions. Only in a condition of freedom from law could human beings express the best qualities of their nature.[18] Rigorous multi-country studies have indeed demonstrated a strong causal connection between inequality and violent crime.[19] On this basis, it would be reasonable to predict that under conditions of greater social equality, levels of violent crime would diminish. But reducing the prevalence of violent crime is not the same as eliminating it entirely. It is difficult to imagine a human community in which ordinary disputes or passionate emotions would never lead to the possibility of a physical confrontation. As political philosopher Jeffrey Reiman has argued, the most basic need for laws and the power to enforce them lies in the recognition that certain forms of behavior – assault, rape, murder – are too dangerous to be left to the judgment of the individual.[20]

As the size and complexity of a community grow, the questions regarding the coordination of intricate social processes in the absence of law and government become more and more difficult to answer. Consider, for example, the ways in which different traditions of political philosophy would treat the issue of social decision rules for a complex operation such as the generation and distribution of electric power to hundreds of thousands or millions of consumers. Classical liberals, such as Smith or Friedman, share with anarchists the desire to coordinate complex social processes on a voluntary basis. This means, of course, that private entrepreneurs should be allowed to respond to consumer demand, buying land, building power plants, and charging customers for electricity as they see fit. Within these privately owned enterprises, the owners of firms will make decisions about operating hours, procedures, supply routes, etc. Within the society as a whole, market competition will coordinate the production and distribution of electricity. Yet liberals find themselves grudgingly forced to accept the existence of a state for at least two reasons. Large-scale markets are difficult to sustain without predictable agreements between transacting parties – thus, market economies depend on governments to recognize and enforce private contracts. Even more fundamentally, the operation of a market economy depends on the existence of private property and therefore on the effective defense of property rights.

Like classical liberals, anarchists suggest that the principle of voluntary association should govern the allocation of resources. In the anarchist community, therefore, power plants and supply grids will be built if people choose to build them. It is unclear, though, how a community without enforceable law would resolve the potential disputes involved with such a large, complex project. If some members of the community favor the construction of a nuclear reactor, while others strongly oppose it, how can the issue be settled? An election could be conducted, although this would assume consensus regarding both voting procedures and acceptance of the outcome. Ultimately, without government, the advocates of nuclear power could not be prevented from building their reactor, nor could their opponents be prevented from sabotaging it.

Even assuming perfect social consensus regarding the construction of a power plant, can we reasonably assume ongoing consensus – every day, every hour – with respect to its operation? Anarchists such as Proudhon insist that within productive enterprises, workers must be free to set their own hours and manage their own activities.[21] Imagine, for example, that an initial consensus among the workers in a power plant leads to a set of operational procedures and safety rules. Either the initial consensus must now be defended by coercive force or we must accept the possibility that, at any moment, any person, acting on any whim, can enter the plant and do as they wish: shut off the supply of power, release toxic chemicals into the atmosphere, etc. If the rules that have been created by consensus are now to be backed by coercive force, we will have reinvented the state and the members of our community will no longer possess absolute individual autonomy. If any breach of consensus means that the rules cannot be enforced, the chances of successfully operating something as complex as an electric power plant look bleak.

For the mainstream of social egalitarian political thought, both the classical liberal and anarchist approaches to complex problems such as a community's desire for electricity vastly underestimate the need for coordination and oversight. The classical liberal reliance on the state only for the defense of property rights allows for the emergence of unacceptable forms of inequality. At a minimum, then, most social egalitarians would argue for government regulation of a privately owned power plant to ensure the rights of its workers and the safety of the surrounding community. But recognizing that electricity is an infrastructural good, most efficiently supplied by one producer (what economists would call a natural monopoly), the mainstream of social egalitarian political philosophy would lean strongly toward the proposal that power plants should be publicly owned and operated for the benefit of the community as a whole. Most social egalitarians, though, would reject the anarchist notion that a publicly owned power plant could be built and operated safely and efficiently without enforceable rules and, therefore, without government.

The social egalitarian approach to decision rules for complex collective endeavors is rooted in its concern with both individual and social access to productive resources. The anarchist tradition, split between its imperatives of unrestricted individual freedom and collective equality, has struggled with this question. For a handful of right-wing anarchists, the Hobbesian nightmare of absolute individual rights to property and a war of all against all is, in fact, a desirable state of affairs. Looking either backward to the open frontier of the Wild West or forward to a post-apocalyptic social collapse, these radical individualists propose to solve the problem of access to productive resources by seizing what they need and defending their claims with a stockpile of weapons.

Most anarchists, though, imagine the good society as a property-less, egalitarian commune, rather than a survivalist bunker. In such a community, access to productive resources would be a universal, collective right. Yet, as we have seen, the ability of such a community to sustain complex economic activity and access to necessary resources without the state depends entirely on the maintenance of consensus among all of its members. Any breakdown of consensus will put either the community's economy or its freedom from law at risk.

One type of anarchist response to this problem is to say that it simply would not arise. Human beings freed from the distorting influence of the state would develop a natural sense of solidarity with one another that would provide the basis for reliable social consensus. Difficult as this is to imagine, it is equally difficult to disprove. Anarchists can always reject appeals to history, arguing that examples of greed or violence serve only to demonstrate human behavior under the influence of repressive laws. But legitimate differences can arise between those with even the best of intentions.

Imagine, for example, a model anarchist economy consisting of a small population and a collectively owned farm that is responsible for producing all of the basic goods needed by the community. Let us say that a dispute arises over the rules under which the land will be farmed. A majority of the community is strongly opposed to the use of pesticides, while a minority believes that careful use of an organically derived pesticide would increase production. The land cannot be divided between the two groups because runoff from the pesticide would affect the untreated acreage. If the majority attempts to prevent the minority from spraying the crops with pesticide, they will have effectively reinvented the state. Yet if the minority proceeds against the will of the majority, they will have effectively reinvented private property. How, then, can unrestricted individual freedom survive if consensus cannot always be assured?

'The individual,' Daniel Guérin suggests, 'owes duties to society only in so far as he has freely consented to become part of it.'[22] The majority within our divided anarchist community could, on this basis, offer the minority a choice: accept our rules or go elsewhere. The anarchist principle of voluntary association, Guérin argues, means that everyone is free to associate or not to associate. Individuals should retain the right to secede from society if they cannot reach agreement with respect to the rules under which it operates.[23]

The individual who secedes from society, however, remains dependent on access to the means of production for life itself and for any measure of realizable freedom. The question that must be posed to the anarchist community, therefore, is not simply 'will individuals have the right to secede?' but rather 'how will individuals or groups who choose to secede continue to get access to productive resources?' If we assume the level of social development to be that of the hunting and gathering economy, the answer is simple: the individual or group choosing to secede from the larger band carries on as before, roaming unclaimed land and consuming freely available resources. The same scenario cannot be duplicated in a world with little unclaimed productive land and large populations of urbanites who could not suddenly revert to a pre-industrial lifestyle.

Individuals or groups choosing to secede from the broader society could hypothetically take with them their portion of the collective means of production, although this, too, presents problems. The land that ultimately supports a highly developed, populous society cannot easily be divided into individual plots representing the amount used to sustain each secessionist. More importantly, the intertwined powers that make high levels of economic development possible cannot easily be unraveled from one another. What, precisely, is the portion of a biotechnology plant that I am owed for having taught one of its employees to read in elementary school? Yet if dissenters are not allowed to secede with productive resources, they are in effect forced to remain members of society by their condition of physical necessity.

The problem faced by anarchists attempting to foster absolute individual freedom by eliminating the state, in other words, is analogous to the problem faced by classical liberals in their claim that the market economy offers both workers and business owners equal freedom. Workers who are able to earn a living only through the sale of labor power to business owners are forced to enter the labor market, just as the members of an anarchist society would be forced to accept majority rule or face starvation. The individual's right under anarchism to secession without productive resources is just as empty as the worker's right under capitalism to become a business owner without investment capital.

Like classical liberals, anarchists seek to provide individuals with a form of negative freedom: the freedom from government. Yet, like liberalism, anarchism ignores the ways in which negative freedom – the freedom to choose – depends upon positive freedom – the availability of material resources and time. In many ways, market economies could be described in precisely the same terms that anarchists such as Goldman use to identify their preferred vision of the future: they are voluntary productive and distributive associations. No law in contemporary American society dictates that there must be a grocery store in my neighborhood. No government official instructs me as to what I must buy there. The existence of this zone of negative freedom, however, does nothing to ensure that the store will have food on its shelves, that the products it sells will be safe, or that I will be able to afford to purchase them.

The absence of government, then, creates three problems for the availability of positive freedom. First, the lack of regulation and co-ordination severely limits the possibilities for economic development and activity. Human history shows a profound correlation between the development of advanced economies and the use of government institutions for economic regulation and coordination. The collapse of largely unregulated capitalist economies in 1929 and the implosion of deregulated financial markets in 2008 demonstrate the extreme instability of classical liberalism's ideal society. Lacking even the ability to support contractual agreements and create durable rules for the use of productive resources, the anarchist society could not reach or sustain even the level of economic development achieved by unregulated capitalism. The freedom such a society could offer would be the freedom experienced by an unemployed person: the freedom to choose from a painfully constricted set of options.

Second, the absence of government radically restricts the supply of public goods. Without formal rules or enforcement power to prevent free-riding, the anarchist society would have no means of ensuring that all members of the community contributed to the provision of collective goods such as roads, schools, or hospitals. It is true that very small communes have been able to sustain collective projects without the need for coercive enforcement. But as societies grow to the point at which their members no longer know one another and are unable to observe each other's behavior directly, it becomes less and less likely that goodwill alone will consistently result in the support needed to maintain the public goods upon which advanced economies – and equal freedom within them – depend.

Third, the stateless society, like the capitalist market economy, is powerless to pursue an egalitarian distribution of meaningful freedom. In the absence of government, we are all political equals. But this form of abstract equality has little meaning in the con-text of significant material inequality. Anarchists such as Proudhon and Goldman recognize this fact, yet in their haste to eliminate the state's support of private property, they would remove the one set of institutions capable of counterbalancing the power of private wealth. It is true that private property exists only because of government's ability to defend it. Yet, in the absence of law, what is to prevent me from accumulating resources, hiring a private army of supporters, and reinventing both government and property? Just as in the world of the marketplace and the private corporation, where government retreats, inequality is free to emerge.

Thus, for the mainstream of the social egalitarian tradition, the abolition of the state is a false path to freedom. Law and government are necessary for the creation of conditions under which real freedom for all can be maximized. State power is needed for the protection of individual rights, for the provision of public goods, and for the coordination of complex economic interactions. But the anarchist tradition is fundamentally correct in its recognition that the existence of a state creates the potential for an imbalance of power between rulers and subjects. The only way to proceed toward social equality, then, is to create a political relationship not between ruler and subject, but between government and citizen. If its values are to be applied consistently, social egalitarianism requires not just any state, but a democratic one.

Political emancipation

Democracy has been described as a political response to the logic of equality.[24] This explains in the most basic sense why a necessary connection exists between democracy and social egalitarianism. But it is equally important to recognize democratic theory as a reaction to the problem posed by individual free will and the legitimacy of self-rule. If, for example, you find yourself alone on an otherwise deserted island, you are likely to go about making decisions regarding your actions and the use of local resources without consulting any higher authorities or bodies of law. Religious believers may contend that in isolation from other human beings they remain bound by divine law, but unless their gods issue them with meticulously detailed lists of daily tasks to be carried out, even the very devout are likely to find themselves taking sole responsibility for many of their choices. Yet if we possess legitimate rights to rule ourselves when in isolation, on what grounds should those rights be diminished when the rescue boat finally returns us to civilization?

Anarchists might respond that there can be no such grounds – that the individual must always be guided only by his or her own will.

The basic political problem that this position fails to account for adequately is the arrangement of hundreds of thousands or millions of individuals with such rights in close proximity to one another. In other words, you may begin to question my right to swing my fist the closer it comes to your nose. On the one hand, if self-ruling individuals are able through their actions to affect the lives of other, similar individuals, the preservation of equal individual rights requires the restriction of certain actions. On the other hand, if self-rule is to remain meaningful, the restrictions imposed on action must ultimately originate with the individual's will.

Since at least the eighteenth century, democratic theory has attempted to cope with this contradiction between the legitimacy of individual self-rule and the necessity of law in a society of self-ruling individuals by drawing a distinction between subjection to another person's arbitrary will and subjection to self-imposed rules.[25] Modern democratic theory will begin from this distinction to suggest that law can legitimately bind members of society, provided that the laws are made through a collective process in which all full members have equal rights to participation.

The requirements for full membership, however, have been objects of contestation in every society that has practiced a form of democratic government. Three such criteria have been the most frequent points of struggle over the definition of citizenship. The question of social identity and, in particular, the distinction between membership and residence in a community is typically central to the distribution of political power. Citizen rights have often been tied to notions of ancestry, or to concepts of race or ethnicity. Everywhere the rights of citizenship are connected to judgments about the possession of reasoning ability. The clearest and most ubiquitous example is the setting of a minimum age for the right to vote, although this is also the basis on which Western electoral democracies excluded adult women from voting rights until the beginning of the twentieth century. The full powers of citizenship have also been allocated in both ancient and modern societies according to the possession of wealth. Until the twentieth century, most electoral democracies (including most American states) restricted voting rights to those who could demonstrate ownership of a certain quantity of property.

Though it has never come easily, classical liberal political thought has proved capable of accommodating more inclusive definitions of citizenship with respect to social identity and more modern judgments concerning rationality. Ultimately, nothing about the concept of race, the notion that reasoning ability differs between the sexes, or the judgment that adulthood begins at eighteen rather than twenty-one years of age, is crucial to liberalism's fundamental values. The question of property rights, however, goes to the heart of classical liberalism's contradictory attitude toward democracy. For liberals, the rights due to individuals in society require the existence of a sphere in which abstractly equal citizens will elect representative lawmakers and press their various claims on government.[26] Yet any government with sufficient power to enforce law will also have the potential to regulate, redistribute, or even abolish private property. The logic of liberalism's belief in individual self-rule leads to its support for democratic government. But the desire to protect private property under conditions of significant material inequality leads liberals to fear what a government elected by the principle of majority rule might do with its power.

Thus, in *On Liberty*, John Stuart Mill agonizes over the possible rise of a tyranny of the majority, under which railways and banks might become pieces of public rather than private property.[27] Restricting voting rights on the basis of wealth is one way of attempting to ensure that an elected government will refrain from using its power to address material inequality, but as a tactic it is also deeply contradictory with classical liberalism's own stated values. The more durable and successful approach to liberal democracy (the combination of elected government and capitalism) has been to erect legal barriers protecting private property from political intervention. Capitalist democracy, in other words, can offer citizenship rights to workers only after the questions of greatest importance to them have been taken off the table. As Ellen Meiksins Wood suggests, in contemporary liberal democracies the scarcity of political goods is overcome through a devaluation of the currency.[28]

Rousseau is perhaps the first modern social egalitarian to warn in stark terms that material inequality will corrode and undermine democratic government.[29] But it is Marx in his early philosophical writings who develops a thoroughgoing critique of the contradiction between political equality and economic inequality. What does it mean, he asks, for electoral democracies to remove property qualifications for the vote? Will it mean, as some liberals fear, that the propertyless will now rule over the propertied?

The state in its own way abolishes distinctions based on birth, rank, education and occupation when it declares birth, rank, education and occupation to be non-political distinctions, when it proclaims that every member of the people is an equal participant in popular sovereignty regardless of these distinctions, when it treats all those elements which go to make up the actual life of the people from the standpoint of the state. Nevertheless the state allows private property, education and occupation to act and assert their particular nature in their own way, i.e., as private property, as education and as occupation.[30]

Upon entering the voting booth, the billionaire investment banker with a degree from Harvard and the dishwasher with a high school education are equals. Their ballots have precisely the same weight and impact on the political process. Yet their different levels of education provide them with different analytical tools and levels of access to information. Their different levels of income provide them with different abilities to support candidates and causes. The different social worlds in which they live offer them different forms of access to officials in government.

Further, to the degree that private property is insulated from government intervention and regulation, the rights possessed by citizens in the political sphere will fail to function in the economic realm. Political scientist Robert Dahl has argued that democracy requires the free election of officials, freedom of expression, alternative sources of information, freedom of association, and inclusive citizenship.[31] Most employees, however, have no right to elect the leaders of their firms. Within the workplace, most employees have no rights to freedom of speech or association. Most employees have no right to see their employers' financial statements. No American today has a right to employment.

The power of private property creates vast zones in which the abstract equality of citizens is effectively meaningless. Its power can be counterbalanced and overcome, but only through political intervention. Equal rights and democratic procedures must be brought to the economic realm from without, by government. Political emancipation – the opening of citizenship rights to all people regardless of sex, ancestry, religion, or wealth – is therefore a real step forward, but an incomplete one.[32]

Social egalitarian democracy

During the last half of the twentieth century, it became common-place for defenders of unregulated capitalism to argue that the goals of social egalitarianism were fundamentally incompatible with the institutions of democracy.[33] Particularly in the USA during the Cold War era, the pursuit of material equality was routinely associated with authoritarian, if not tyrannical, government.

Social egalitarianism and democracy, however, have a long history of interconnection and symbiotic development. Just as eighteenth- and nineteenth-century liberals feared that democratic government would threaten the power of accumulated wealth, European social egalitarians organizing in the wake of the Industrial Revolution assumed that once it had been stripped of property qualifications, electoral democracy would ultimately lead to economic transforma-tions benefiting ordinary working people. Thus, in the *Communist Manifesto*, Marx and Engels declared that the first step in a workers' revolution would be the achievement of 'victory for democracy.'[34] Years later, in an analysis of the German Social Democratic Party's platform, Engels wrote: 'If one thing is certain it is that our party and the working class can only come to power under the form of a democratic republic.'[35] As August Nimtz has made clear in his careful analysis of their political activism, Marx and Engels stood at the center of the nineteenth-century movement for democracy.[36]

The strong connection between electoral democracy and egalit-arian economic transformation is clear in the German Social Demo-cratic Party's 1891 program. The platform centered on three sets of demands: democratic reform of government (universal voting rights for all adults, election of judges, and the separation of Church and state), regulation of the market economy (limitation of working hours, improvement of working conditions, and the right to collective bargaining), and investment in public goods (public legal assistance, medical care, education, and insurance).[37] The connections can also be seen more broadly in the rise of European socialist parties and the achievement of universal manhood suffrage. In nearly all of the western European states, the founding of a major socialist party in the late 1800s was followed by the opening of voting rights to working-class men at the turn of the century.[38]

The anomalies that would decisively reshape the perceived relation-ship between social egalitarianism and democracy were, of course, the Bolshevik revolution and the formation of the Soviet Union.

The revolution brought with it a system of one-party government, an example that was to be followed by revolutionary movements in the underdeveloped world for years to come. From 1924 to 1953, political power in the USSR came to be even more tightly centralized and personalized under the leadership of Joseph Stalin. After Stalin's death, Nikita Khrushchev attempted to reverse course, but was pushed aside by more conservative leaders who remained at the helm until the 1980s. By the time that Mikhail Gorbachev launched the next major effort at political reform, the Soviet socialist project was beyond repair.

Historians and political scientists battled throughout the twentieth century over the reasons for the Soviet Union's political trajectory. Explanations of the USSR's authoritarian character focused on the exigencies of a revolutionary seizure of power, the tyrannical intentions of individual leaders, the demands imposed by economic underdevelopment and industrialization, and the effects of international pressure exerted by the West. For political philosophers, the questions posed by the Soviet experience centered on the relationship between social egalitarianism and democracy. The most strident right-wing critics continually pointed to the USSR as evidence that any effort to use government institutions for the promotion of social equality would lead to dictatorship. Such arguments, however, were unable to account for the experience of the Scandinavian countries in which social egalitarian economic policies had been pursued by democratically elected governments for decades. In western Europe and North America, many on the left strenuously maintained that the Soviet experience bore no relationship to their political values. Socialism meant democracy, therefore the Soviet Union's lack of democracy meant that it could not be considered a socialist country.

The problem with both positions was their shared fixation on the notion of 'socialism' as an all-encompassing package of political, economic, and cultural institutions. Critics on both the right and the left, in other words, failed to see the trees for the forest. The Soviet Union's tremendous investment in public education, transportation, and healthcare, as well as its guarantee of the right to employment, was clearly expressive of social egalitarian values; its centralization of political power in the hands of a relatively small cadre of party leaders was not. For politicians and commentators on the right, the image of a falsely totalized 'socialism' in which each element was inseparably joined to the others was enormously useful. Any fault that could be found in the USSR could immediately be applied to any policy proposal emanating from the political left. Yet, in their efforts to defend the good name of socialism by insisting that it had nothing whatsoever to do with the Soviet experience, the Western left increasingly pushed its own political vision into the realm of utopian fantasy. For a time, 'socialism' came to stand for the achievement of untarnished social perfection. Eventually, it began to stand for nothing at all.

If in the East social egalitarian economic policies failed to guarantee democratic politics, in the West electoral democracy failed to guarantee egalitarian economics. During the twentieth century, socialist parties were able to find their way into power throughout western Europe, although as they did so, they found themselves either willing or able to accomplish far less than what many expected of them. The failure of western European socialist parties to achieve more dramatic forms of economic transformation – wholesale nationalization of industry or sweeping redistributions of wealth – has been attributed by some prominent political scientists to an insurmountable dilemma confronting the electoral road to social egalitarianism: any government elected to power in a society with a largely capitalist economy will become dependent upon capitalism for its own survival.[39] Voters are powerfully motivated by their own economic wellbeing and frequent elections mean that government officials will have little time in which to produce positive results before being turned out of office. Thus, as Adam Przeworski has argued, social egalitarian parties elected to government tend to abandon plans for sweeping economic transformation and settle instead for cooperation with capitalists in increasing productivity and distributing the proceeds.[40]

There is a powerful logic to Przeworski's argument, although it fails to explain significant variations in the promotion of social egalitarian values in different countries at different points in their history. During the twentieth century, more progress was made toward social egalitarianism in the Scandinavian countries than in the rest of western Europe. During the same period, more progress was made toward social egalitarian values in the whole of western Europe than in the USA. In the whole of the industrialized world, more progress was made toward social egalitarian values between the 1940s and the 1970s than during the 1980s and 1990s. Electoral democracy clearly did not bring about the total transformation that many on both the left and the right imagined 'socialism' to be. Yet the degree to which

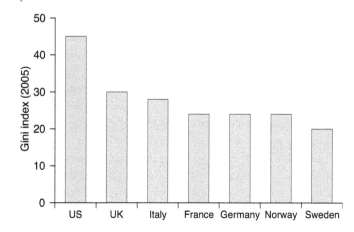

FIGURE 4.1 Gini index of income inequality, 2005
Sources: US Census Bureau, Historical Income Tables A-3; *CIA World Factbook*, 'Distribution of family income, Gini index,' www.cia. gov/library/publications/the-world-factbook/fields/2172.html

the western European socialist parties changed their societies has often been underestimated. Focusing exclusively on the question of industrial nationalization, we can miss the importance for ordinary working people of economic regulation (limitation of working hours, minimum wage requirements, anti-discrimination laws, health and safety regulations) and the provision of public goods (education, healthcare, unemployment and retirement insurance).

The one highly industrialized country in which a large electoral socialist party failed to emerge – the USA – lags far behind all of the European states in the legal rights and public goods offered to ordinary working people. European workers enjoy stronger forms of job security, longer paid vacations, and vastly more generous systems of publicly funded healthcare, unemployment insurance, and retirement income than do their American counterparts. The overall effect of these differences is reflected in the levels of material inequality found on either side of the Atlantic (Figure 4.1).

It must be said, however, that the experiences of the western European electoral socialist parties have always raised crucial questions regarding the relationship between social egalitarianism and democracy. Social egalitarianism's most fundamental value – maximum equal freedom for all – cannot be reconciled with an undemocratic form of government. Revolutionary leaders have often argued that in the heat of battle, authority must be tightened and centralized – just as it must be in any other type of military conflict. But the broad tradition of social egalitarian political philosophy has always maintained that material equality was to be added to legal and political equality, not exchanged for them. Yet, if the form of electoral democracy that arose side by side with capitalist economies failed to guarantee social equality, could it be that social equality required its own specific form of democratic institutions?

Political outcomes in a democracy are never guaranteed for the simple reason that the interests of citizens are neither self-evident nor free-standing – they are shaped in part by the political process itself. The fact that I find myself unemployed or earning too little to meet my needs does not tell me how best to change the situation or what role government should play in the solution. The existence of significant material inequality will mean that calls for government regulation of private industry or the provision of public goods are likely to be opposed by powerful campaigns funded by wealthy donors. Further, in the real world of democratic politics, policy proposals rarely appear in isolation from one another. Instead, economic questions are bundled together with approaches to foreign policy and images of national, racial, religious, or cultural identity under the aegis of particular parties or candidates.

It is equally true, though, that no system of democratic government is so simplistic as to create an unmediated translation of popular will into policy. Institutions of government contain biases favoring certain interests and values, not only by accident, but by design. Constitutions offer the clearest example. Their purpose is to prevent even democratically elected governments from engaging in certain actions. The US constitution's protection of free speech is meant to limit the ability of citizens and their elected representatives to restrict expression, even if it is their will to do so. Constitutional protections of private property act in the same way to limit and shape democratic outcomes. It is in this context that we should understand Marx's comment that 'the working class cannot simply lay hold of the ready-made state machinery, and wield it for its own purposes.'[41] The institutions of government that have evolved in the midst of capitalist economies have been honed to fit capitalism's requirements. The pursuit of social equality may well require radically different institutional forms.

The emergence of democracy in ancient Athens suggests a useful example of institutional transformation as a response to the contradiction between political equality and material inequality. The centerpiece of Athenian democracy was, of course, the assembly – the seat of sovereign power at which adult male citizens practiced a form of direct, participatory debate and legislation. After 487 BCE, government offices needed for implementation of the law between assemblies were assigned to citizens by a lottery, further decentralizing political power.[42] But Athenian democrats clearly recognized that rights to political participation were empty unless material circumstances made actual participation possible. If citizens could not afford to leave the occupations from which they made their living to serve in government, the right to hold office was effectively meaningless. Thus, one of the key reforms secured by supporters of the Athenian democracy was payment for government service. The introduction of state pay for service in government offices or on juries ensured that wealth did not determine the real ability of citizens to participate in the political process.[43]

The Athenian form of direct democracy is clearly the model from which Rousseau draws inspiration in *The Social Contract*, whose well-known opening line makes plain his central concern with the issue of equal freedom: 'Man is born free, and everywhere he is in chains.'[44] Rousseau begins his most famous meditation on politics and government from the central contradiction confronted by all forms of democratic theory: the capacities of reason and free will provide us with the bases for a legitimate claim to self-rule, yet unless we live in isolation, we must somehow share that right with others whose claims to self-rule are just as defensible as our own. Rousseau is no anarchist. He sees formal law and government as necessary means for the protection of rights and goods. But as a committed egalitarian, Rousseau is determined to find a political form in which the individual's right to self-rule can meaningfully coexist with the power of the state.[45]

That form of politics, Rousseau argues, would be a type of participatory democracy in which citizen assemblies held sovereign power. Between meetings of the assembly, government institutions would hold executive authority, but at the opening of each assembly, the first agenda items would offer citizens the chance to alter the form of government or to replace its officers.[46] Rousseau is clear about the fact, however, that such office-holders would be in no way similar to the elected legislators characteristic of parliamentary democracy:

> Sovereignty cannot be represented for the same reason that it cannot

be alienated. It consists essentially in the general will, and the will does not allow of being represented [...] The English people believes itself to be free. It is greatly mistaken; it is free only during the election of the members of Parliament. Once they are elected, the populace is enslaved; it is nothing. The use the English people makes of that freedom in the brief moments of its liberty certainly warrants their losing it.[47]

For Rousseau, the form of state in which equal freedom could be achieved would require the direct participation of citizens in shaping and agreeing to legislation, rather than the election of representatives.

Marx suggests something similar in his comments on the Paris Commune – the temporary seizure of power by a working-class uprising in 1871. While the Commune's municipal councilors were chosen by election, they remained under revocable mandate and were paid average workers' wages. The model of representatives bound by clear, revocable mandates, directly responsible to their constituents, Marx argues, announced a crucial break with the form of parliamentary democracy then emerging under capitalism:

> Instead of deciding once in three or six years which member of the ruling class to misrepresent the people in Parliament, universal suffrage was to serve the people, constituted in Communes, as individual suffrage serves every other employer in the search for the workmen and managers in his business.[48]

Although it survived only a few months, Marx maintained that the Commune was nothing less than 'the political form at last discovered under which to work out the economic emancipation of labor.'[49]

It comes as a surprise to many that Vladimir Lenin strongly agreed with Marx on this point. The perception of Lenin as an autocrat, of course, owes much to Cold War propaganda and to an intentional blurring of the lines between Lenin and Stalin. There is no questioning the fact that as a revolutionary leader, Lenin argued for military discipline in the heat of battle, but his concept of 'democratic centralism' has often been badly misinterpreted as applying to ordinary political life. Lenin does maintain that in the midst of a revolutionary struggle, an organization should be able to unify behind a decision after conducting an open debate. Nowhere, though, does he suggest that similar procedures should apply to the normal course of democratic governance.[50]

The main text in which Lenin addresses the question of post-revolutionary government draws heavily on Marx's analysis of the Paris Commune and reiterates the argument for a model of non-parliamentary democratic practice. In *State and Revolution*, Lenin distinguishes himself from the anarchists, maintaining that law and government will continue to be necessary in a highly developed society, and from Rousseau, contending that elected representation will be unavoidable. The model of democracy he envisions for the egalitarian society, however, is one in which representatives would conduct their work under mandates from their constituents, to whom they would regularly report back. The role of state officials in this form of democracy, he argues, would be reduced to that of responsible, revocable, modestly paid foremen and accountants.[51]

Both direct, participatory democracy and mandated representation suggest an effort by political philosophers to navigate between two obstacles threatening social equality in the practice of democratic politics. On the one hand, weak or nonexistent law will permit unchecked inequality and exploitation. On the other hand, distant, unresponsive government creates its own form of inequality between office-holders and citizens. Direct democracy is clearly the more radical approach and Rousseau's sharp criticism of elected representation makes plain his intention to ensure both effective law and the political empowerment of citizens. Yet there is a strong resemblance between his model of direct democracy and the system of mandated representation proposed by Marx and Lenin. Between meetings of Rousseau's assembly, citizens are in effect represented by the government officials chosen to oversee implementation of the law. It is clear, though, from his underscoring of the assembly's power to alter the composition of government, that Rousseau intends for its office-holders to operate under strict, revocable mandates. Marx and Lenin do not envision citizens making law directly as Rousseau does, but they too suggest the need for linkages between citizens and representatives going beyond those of the liberal democratic parliament.

The models of radical democracy that would transcend the limits of liberal parliamentary practice, however, face at least three serious problems when combined with the other features of large, highly developed societies. First, as populations grow larger, direct democracy becomes inefficient to the point of impossibility. Technology can be used to overcome communication and information challenges, but the process of legislation in a contemporary society would not become any less time-consuming. Direct democracy, with citizen assemblies responsible for lawmaking, would require the greatest commitment of time and effort, although any system of meetings designed to equip representatives with popular mandates would put heavy demands on citizens' time. It is entirely possible that the low voter participation rates (barely over 50 percent in US presidential elections) are reflective of citizens' indifference to a process that seems relatively distant from the actual levers of power. But it is equally possible that the strongest advocates of participatory democracy may overestimate the willingness of most citizens to spend their time in committee meetings.

Second, in any society that had not already achieved significant progress toward material equality, mechanisms designed to empower citizens would be vulnerable to being hijacked by wealthy individuals or corporations. California's ballot initiative system offers an instructive example. Created during the progressive era as a means of counterbalancing the power of private industry, ballot initiatives allow citizens to vote on new laws directly, bypassing the state legislature. But the use of paid signature-gatherers to qualify proposals for the ballot and mass media advertising campaigns to attract support for them has turned the initiative system into another channel through which accumulated wealth can be used to influence the political process.

This suggests a third, broader point that must be underscored. It is false to assume that in a large, highly developed society majority preferences will always tend in an egalitarian direction. Democratic government is necessary for the pursuit of social equality, but it is not sufficient. In practice, the greatest progress toward social egalitarian values has been achieved not by government officials or representatives acting alone, but by governments influenced by organizations and movements in the wider society. The role played by labor unions and political parties outside of government cannot be overlooked. The transformation of formal democratic institutions can help to shift political outcomes in an egalitarian direction, but it cannot guarantee such outcomes. Social egalitarianism, like any other set of political values, must be fought for continually through the mechanisms of formal democracy.

FIVE

Internationalism

Every political question either poses or presumes the question of membership. Equal rights under the law are afforded to members of a defined community. Opportunities to share in the practice of democratic governance are similarly offered to those grouped within demarcated boundaries. Yet the everyday familiarity of the political units in which we live sometimes allows them to fade from careful scrutiny. We often assume that our debates about politics refer to cities, regions, or nation-states, taking for granted the prior questions of their borders and terms of inclusion. Since the nineteenth century, however, social egalitarian political philosophy has been uniquely attuned to the question of membership and this question alone has sometimes been sufficient to divide the social egalitarian tradition from others.

On what basis should the borders of a political community be drawn? A commonsense approach might suggest that the boundaries of law and government should correspond with the natural independence of self-sustaining social and economic units. Technological and economic development, however, have long since obliterated any such autonomy, even for the largest of nation-states. In 2007, the USA imported and exported more than $3.9 trillion worth of goods and services.[1] A large portion of the energy resources upon which the US economy depends comes from outside of its political borders, as does an ever-expanding range of basic consumer goods. In this sense, it is difficult to conceive of the USA or any of its international trading partners as economically independent.

But it is not just the contemporary expansion of global trade that poses questions for the naturalness of national boundaries. Nation-states are always political inventions, the result of self-conscious projects to weld together expanses of territory and masses of people, and to provide them with unifying forms of collective identity: names, songs, flags, sports teams. This does not mean that the emotional sentiments fed by nationalist projects are tenuous or insubstantial. On the contrary, they have been among the most powerful emotions to appear in modern history, often shading into sentiments of national chauvinism, xenophobia, and racism. One of the first scholars to comment on the phenomenon of early modern nationalism, the philosopher Johann Gottfried von Herder, noted in the enthusiastic celebration of exclusive identity a tendency toward the feeling that 'whoever is not with us and of us, is below us.'[2]

There is good reason, then, for those upholding the value of equality to question exclusive forms of national identity. In their own way, of course, the captains of industry maintain a practical distance from the belief in nation above all else. 'To be in business,' the chairman of a Canadian-owned auto parts manufacturer with production lines in Mexico once stated, 'your first mandate is to make money, and money has no heart, soul, conscience, homeland.'[3] To reiterate, though, the movement of capital across nation-state boundaries is nothing new. As early as 1776, Adam Smith had already identified specialization, trade, and interdependence as the principles that would drive the expansion of market economies. By 1848, Marx and Engels had recognized capitalism's emergence as a global economic system.

Responding to this reality, nineteenth- and twentieth-century social egalitarians developed concepts of international working-class solidarity and universal membership. Such forms of identity were not easy to sustain, particularly when pitted against robust forms of nationalism. Internationalism often became a pious ideal, rather than a living practice.[4] Yet in order to grasp the ways in which social egalitarians conceive of rights, responsibilities, and the possibilities for human freedom, it is important to understand the development of social egalitarian internationalism. Why was it that egalitarians like Marx believed so strongly in a political transcendence of the nation-state and under what conditions did transnational forms of political identity begin to take shape?

The founders

If the years between the late eighteenth and middle nineteenth centuries in Europe were, as Benedict Anderson has described them, 'the dusk of religion and the dawn of nationalism,' what this image would seem to neglect is the birth, during the latter half of this period, of nationalism's self-conscious alternative, internationalism.[5] Of the two, nationalism was clearly the dominant force. Early European nationalism, as Eric Hobsbawm has argued, was not only a self-conscious ideological project, but a pervasive and near-mystical belief in the logical necessity of nations defined by culture, ethnicity, and language.[6] That belief, as Hobsbawm rightfully emphasizes, must be set against the historical fact that no nation-state came into being as the expression of a natural and necessary identity. In 1857, the epitome of self-conscious European nationalism, Giuseppe Mazzini, drew up an ideal map of Europe consisting of eleven nation-states. Sixty-two years later, presiding over a systematic redrawing of the boundaries of European states, Woodrow Wilson proposed a map composed of no fewer than twenty-six sovereign states.[7] On the one hand, the self-conscious ideology of nationalism was necessarily an exclusive project, staking a claim to self-determination as against other nations. On the other hand, within the early European nationalist movements, particularly the 'Young Europe' groupings founded or influenced by Mazzini, the nationalist project implied a certain type of transnational solidarity: all nations struggling to be born were perceived to be working toward a common objective and were therefore comrades in arms. But, following a trajectory that would be repeated just over a century later in the disintegration of pan-Africanism, as nationalist movements won their struggles for sovereignty, such latent internationalist sentiments fell by the wayside.

It was in the nineteenth-century social egalitarian movement that internationalist political thought took firm root, with Marx and Engels being responsible for the decisive intervention. Marx's political vision, in particular, is striking for its refusal to be bound by national frontiers. There are moments in Marx's early work in which he ruminates on the nature of national differences, but even these are shot through with transnational concerns. In an article written in 1844 he refers to the specific nature of national working classes. 'The German proletariat,' he writes, 'is the theoretician of the European proletariat just as the English proletariat is its economist and the French its politician.'[8] There is clearly a recognition here of historical and institutional differences, breaking along the boundaries of nation-states. Yet the unifying concern is transnational. Whatever their differences, the three national working classes are understood to be connected, and connected by more than just the happenstance of their class positions. The English proletariat had something to gain from the experiences of the French and the Germans (and vice versa) because certain of their needs, goals, and interests were the same.

Thus, the specter invoked in the opening line of the *Communist Manifesto* haunted neither Germany, nor France, nor England, but

Europe. In a pamphlet meant to clarify the aims and ideals of the organization they had recently joined, Marx and Engels gave special prominence to the idea of a transnational political practice:

> Communists are distinguished from the rest of the proletarian parties only in that, on the one hand, in the various national struggles of the proletarians they raise and highlight the common interests of the whole proletariat, independent of nationality, and on the other hand, in the various stages of development through which the struggle between proletariat and bourgeoisie proceeds, they always represent the interests of the movement as a whole.[9]

They went on to make what is surely the most famous statement of political internationalism to date. Refuting critics who charge that communists would seek to abolish nations and nationalism, they respond that 'Workers have no nation of their own. We cannot take from them what they do not have.'[10]

The usual interpretation of this passage holds that Marx and Engels would have been baffled by expressions of working-class nationalism. Roman Szporluk, for example, argues that Marx 'did not envisage the proletariat succumbing to nationalistic temptations proffered by the bourgeoisie.'[11] The significance of national political entities for Marx's vision of social egalitarianism, however, goes much farther than the question of whether or not the proletariat was capable of being swayed by a nationalistic appeal. The 'world-historical role' of the proletariat, he maintained, 'is not a question of what this or that proletarian, or even the whole proletariat itself, imagines to be the goal for the moment.'[12] Internationalism was both a philosophical and a strategic element of Marx's political thought, but it was not a matter of mass faith.

The roots of Marx's political thought lie in his twin critiques of alienation and political emancipation. Citizenship in the modern liberal state was, on this account, at once a genuine political victory and a cruel joke. Universal citizenship blazed the way forward and at the same time offered only a hollow version of its own promise. Citizens in the liberal state were now free and equal as abstract political beings, while remaining 'the playthings of alien powers' in every other aspect of daily life.[13] The implications of this position become clearer in Marx's consideration of the Irish question during the 1840s. Though unequivocally maintaining that English rule over Ireland was 'the most abominable reign of terror and the most reprehensible corruption,' he saw no solution to the situation in the creation of an independent Irish state. Its small size and economic underdevelopment would leave it mired in poverty and subject to the dictates of capital if not to those of the Crown.[14] The firming-up of a national boundary between England and Ireland, then, could release the grasp of one alien power, while another – equally alien and equally oppressive – would remain comfortably in place.

But the limited capacity of the nation-state to deliver a meaningful form of emancipation from the whims of alien power was not only a concern for the underdeveloped and the colonized. As capital expanded to create a global market, an increasingly broad section of humanity would ultimately find itself in the same position as the Irish found themselves vis-à-vis Britain:

> In history up to the present it is certainly an empirical fact that separate individuals have, with the broadening of their activity into world-historical activity, become more and more enslaved under a power alien to them (a pressure which they have conceived of as a dirty trick on the part of the so-called universal spirit, etc.), a power which has become more and more enormous and, in the last instance, turns out to be the world market.[15]

As the power of privately owned capital grew to global proportions, the working class would increasingly be forced to act on a world scale. The claim made here is not that workers were somehow incapable of thinking in the register of nationalism, but that a failure to transcend the boundaries of the nation-state in their political practice would impose restrictive limits on the victories that they could achieve.

After the revolutions of 1848 and the subsequent restoration of old orders across Europe, two new, primarily tactical elements were added to Marx's internationalism. The first was a recognition that one national revolution could ignite others, both through the material connections between nation-states and by demonstration effect. The second was the confirmed knowledge that even simultaneous national revolutions which remained isolated from one another stood little chance of survival. The vulnerability of a lone social revolution was clearly demonstrated, if not by the defeat of the revolutions of 1848, by the massacre of the Paris Commune. Yet the real weakness Marx perceived in national social revolutions lay not in their ability to field troops, but in finding themselves adrift in a world dominated by the economic might of capital:

Just as the workers thought they would be able to emancipate themselves side by side with the bourgeoisie, so they thought they would be able to consummate a proletarian revolution within the national walls of France, side by side with the remaining bourgeois nations. But French relations of production are conditioned by the foreign trade of France, by her position on the world market and the laws thereof; how was France to break them without a European revolutionary war, which would strike back at the despot of the world market, England?[16]

'England,' he concluded, 'seems to be the rock on which revolutionary waves are shattered, where the new society perishes in its mother's lap.'[17] National revolutions could lay hands only on national institutions and instruments of power. Capital, however, refused to be bound by the fictions of nationality. It was – and was becoming increasingly – transnational.

For all that has been said about the inaccuracy of Marx's predictions and the obsolescence of his economic thought, his descriptions, circa 1848, of the globalization of capitalism are strikingly familiar in our own time:

> The need for a constantly expanding outlet for their products pursues the bourgeoisie over the whole world. It must get a foothold everywhere, settle everywhere, establish connections everywhere. It forces all nations to adopt the bourgeois mode of production or go under; it forces them to introduce so-called civilization amongst themselves, i.e. to become bourgeois. In a phrase, it creates a world in its own image.[18]

But as his assessment of the struggle and defeat in France had pointed out, the globalization of production, consumption, and finance meant more than just the proliferation of capitalism as a national way of life. The existence of capitalism as a set of transnational relationships, rather than as an evolutionary path to be followed by each nation in its turn, meant that a social egalitarian movement would have to be able to operate internationally.

It was this point, as Marx argued in the *Critique of the Gotha Program*, that the German workers' movement had failed to comprehend. Its internationalism, reflected in the proposed founding documents of the German Social Democratic Workers' Party, went no farther than a vision of fraternal peace between nations once each national working class had risen to power. Not only did this go no farther than bourgeois notions of 'world peace,' it failed to rise even to the level of capitalism's own globalization:

> In fact the commitment to internationalism in the programme is infinitely less than that of even the free-traders. They also claim that their efforts will be 'the international brotherhood of all nations'. But they are also doing something to internationalise trade, and are in no way satisfied in the knowledge that all nations are engaged in commerce at home.[19]

It would not be enough (as in the language of contemporary political slogans) to 'think globally and act locally.' Internationalism, for Marx, was not a matter of kind sentiments, but a crucial strategic element for the social egalitarian movement.

From the Second to the Third International

The Second International, founded in 1889 at the International Workers' Congress in Paris, continued to reflect tensions over the real meaning and content of internationalism. Issues such as colonialism and immigration sparked debate over the proper response to transnational dynamics, but the questions that would ultimately collapse the International – national militarism and war – were already on the agenda as early as the 1907 Stuttgart conference. There, the lines were drawn between August Bebel and Gustave Hervé: Bebel upholding the rights of national self-determination; Hervé arguing for an uncompromising internationalist anti-militarism. For Bebel, culture and progress were rooted in national freedom and independence. Defensive wars could therefore be justified to the extent that they protected what the proletariat ultimately stood to inherit: the Fatherland.[20] To this, Hervé responded that the defensive war was an illusion offering little clear guidance in an increasingly tense political environment:

> Bebel has most obligingly informed me that fatherlands exist today in Europe as a historical fact [...] But I ask you: When the German soldiers are sent off to reestablish the throne of the Russian tsar, when Prussia and France attack the proletarians, what will you do? Please do not answer with metaphysics and dialectics, but openly and clearly; practically and tactically, what will you do?[21]

The International resolved to make every effort to prevent the outbreak of war and, in its event, to work toward its immediate end,

making appropriate use along the way of the political crisis it was
sure to precipitate. As is well known, when the moment of decision
came, most of the International's affiliated parties followed exactly
the opposite course.

Once World War I had broken out, with nearly all of the European
socialists backing their national war efforts, Karl Kautsky produced
a refined version of Bebel's position, adding to it the concept of an
internationalist patriotism. In practice, he admitted, internationalist patriotism might be difficult to differentiate from nationalist or
chauvinist varieties, but its distinctiveness lay in its ultimate vision
of international solidarity:

> Each people, and the proletariat of each country as well, has an
> urgent interest in preventing the enemy of its country from crossing
> its frontiers, since that would convert the horror and devastation
> of war into its most terrible form, an enemy invasion. And in each
> national state the proletariat must also commit its full energy to
> assure that the independence and unity of the national territory
> remains intact. That is a fundamental part of democracy, which in
> turn is the necessary basis for the proletariat's struggle and victory.[22]

Internationalism, in this version, had specific meaning only in peace-
time. Once national armies were arranged in the field against one
another, socialist internationalism was to be traded for the expedients
of national defense. Like the Lassallean authors of the Gotha Program, Kautsky conceived of internationalism as the fraternal relations
between national parties primarily occupied with national political
struggles. Upon winning power they might all get along amicably, but
social equality was first and foremost a national project.

Kautsky's opponents were few, but they were some of European
social democracy's most brilliant minds. Among them, Rosa Luxemburg replied with a savage parody of internationalist patriotism:

> The world historic call of the *Communist Manifesto* has been
> substantially enriched and, as corrected by Kautsky, now reads:
> 'Proletarians of all countries, unite in peacetime and cut each other's
> throats in wartime!' Today our slogan is: 'May every bullet find
> a Russian; every bayonet a Frenchman.' Tomorrow, after peace is
> declared, it will be: 'We embrace the millions of the whole world.'[23]

Above all, the experiences of the slide into war convinced leaders
such as Luxemburg, Lenin, and Trotsky of the need for international

political action rather than simply fraternal solidarity between national parties.

As post-war revolutions broke out in eastern and central Europe, two points noted by Marx in the wake of 1848 were once again underscored. First, national revolutions had international effects. The Bolshevik revolution in Russia provided the inspiration and the models of organization for the rising in Germany less than a year later. Second, an isolated national revolution stood little chance of survival. About the latter point, the Bolshevik leaders were clear. Arguments both for and against the seizure of power in Russia were made in the context of forecasts predicting a revolution in Germany.

'At all events,' Lenin maintained, 'under all conceivable circumstances, if the German revolution does not come, we are doomed.'[24] On the one hand, as Lenin (and later Antonio Gramsci) pointed out, Russia's lack of development facilitated revolution. On the other hand, once the more developed countries had succeeded in revolution, Russia would follow rather than lead. 'Perhaps we are making mistakes,' Lenin conceded in an address to the Eighth Party Congress, 'but we hope that the proletariat of the West will correct them. And we appeal to the European proletariat to help us in our work.'[25]

From the beginning of World War I, socialist critics of the Second International argued for the creation of a new organization, stressing two ways in which it should differ from the collapsed body. First, it would need binding power over its member parties. An International that could pass resolutions against militarism only to have its affiliates march off to opposing trenches was useless. Second, it would have to develop a genuine capacity for international action. In this new vision, internationalism was to be a way of practicing revolutionary politics rather than an ultimate ideal of world peace.

The Third or Communist International was founded in Moscow in 1919, but like the Bolshevik revolution, it waited for Germany. The only German delegate at the Comintern's founding conference had been instructed by his party to oppose the premature formation of a new International. While supporting the initiative in principle, the Germans wanted to be sure that a new International would have sufficient forces with which to support the social egalitarian struggle. Only the late arrival of a delegate from Austria and his presentation of a highly optimistic picture of the chances for revolution in central Europe convinced the conference to proceed with the Comintern's founding.[26]

It has been a common practice among many historians and political scientists to treat the Third International as nothing more than an instrument of national foreign policy for the USSR, but while Stalin's turn toward the vision of 'socialism in one country' unquestionably drove the Third International in this direction, we cannot make sense of its wider ideological effects without accounting for the fact that most of those who belonged to its affiliated organizations continued to adhere to a radically different political vision. Through the 1930s, a wedge was increasingly driven between those who identified with the stated goals of the International and those whose loyalties were exclusive to Stalin and his inner circle.[27] Herein lies the reason for the marked tension in the Executive Committee of the Communist International (ECCI) when considering the outbreak of the Spanish Civil War in 1936. Although the ECCI formally recommended taking action to support the Left Popular Front government under siege by Franco's troops, it did so knowingly risking an accusation of 'Trotsky-ism' – a charge the recent executions of Zinoviev and Kamenev had proved perilous in the extreme.[28]

The International Brigades

In September 1936, the Comintern's affiliate parties in Europe were instructed to begin recruiting volunteers to fight in Spain.[29] The American Communist Party was brought into the effort three months later.[30] By the end of the war, the total number of those who had joined the International Brigades had reached 35,000. Most of the volunteers were European nationals, but at least four thousand came from the United States and Canada, and a few even reached Spain from as far away as Mexico and South America. If the collapse of the Second International into opposed warring sides marked the low point of socialist internationalism, the organization of a military force consisting of volunteers from around the world united by political principle was surely its height. At least one historian has argued that the Comintern's involvement in the organization of the Brigades was unnecessary.[31] Yet the number of otherwise unaffiliated volunteers who joined the International Brigades was far lower than those connected to communist parties and youth organizations.[32] Travel to Spain from the United States and from France was illegal during the war and under any circumstances it was costly. Only the organizational infrastructure of the communist parties, their collective resources, and their experience in underground work made such an operation possible. Tickets for volunteers coming from overseas were paid for by the party, though in most cases this cost was eventually reimbursed by the Spanish government. Once in France, an elaborate network of party members and sympathizers housed and fed the volunteers and transported them across the border.[33]

At a purely organizational level, the existence of that infrastructure made the International Brigades possible. Yet we should also note the more subtle (though perhaps even more significant) ways in which the nature of the Comintern created the possibility of such an unlikely political event. The American volunteers of the Abraham Lincoln Battalion (to take just one example) came from a wide variety of class and educational backgrounds. Most came from large urban areas, but by the end of the war virtually all sections of the country were represented.[34] What they had in common was a sense of participation in a transnational political struggle. 'When the crisis broke,' one volunteer recalled, 'we were ready.'[35]

That sense of readiness could not have come from the course of events itself. Millions of others also knew of what was happening in Spain but did not for a moment consider making the journey to join in the fight. For the majority of those who volunteered, the readiness to do so – the ability to see the Spanish war as something of direct relevance to them – came from the ways in which mass-based Comintern affiliates were able to give a transnational political vision immediate and concrete content. Particularly for those in cities with large Communist Party and Young Communist League communities, such as New York, an internationalist political identity had become a meaningful part of everyday life. As a form of ideology, in other words, internationalism had become a lived practice.

From internationalism to foreign aid

A more contemporary example of internationalist political practice can be seen in the support for organized resistance to apartheid in South Africa. After the early 1960s, as an exiled organization, the African National Congress (ANC) became entirely dependent on support from foreign governments and solidarity organizations for its survival. Nelson Mandela's tour of the newly independent African states in 1962 won promises of assistance, although the leaders of those states had little ability to deliver. Economically, the decolonized countries were weak, and those sharing a border with South Africa had little capacity to resist any military pressure it might choose to apply. Thus, the bulk of support for the exiled ANC came from the Soviet Union, East Germany, and the Scandinavian social democracies. On the one hand, Soviet aid for the anti-apartheid struggle was driven by the Khrushchev era's sense of socialist renewal.[36] On the other hand, such efforts were increasingly ad hoc and conceived of as foreign aid rather than as the pursuit of socialist internationalism. Likewise, while the ANC won the backing of a broad and highly effective international anti-apartheid movement, that campaign's ideological foundation was, in the main, one of moral solidarity with a foreign cause, rather than transnational political struggle toward a common goal.

Few ANC documents produced either during the years in exile or after the organization's return to South Africa attempt to place the anti-apartheid struggle in any wider international context. The 'Revolutionary Programme' document adopted at the 1969 Morogoro Conference referred to internationalism as a long-term goal, but one which in the short run had to be put aside in favor of the clearer objectives of nationalism:

> In the last resort it is only the success of the national democratic
> revolution which – by destroying the existing social and economic
> relationships – will bring with it a correction of the historical
> injustices perpetrated against the indigenous majority and thus lay
> the basis for a new and deeper internationalist approach. Until then,
> the national sense of grievance is the most potent revolutionary
> force which must be harnessed. To blunt it in the interest of abstract
> concepts of internationalism, is, in the long run, doing neither a
> service to revolution nor to internationalism.[37]

There is surely an echo here of Frantz Fanon's denunciation of those in and around the anti-colonial struggles of the 1950s and 1960s who might have criticized the limitations of nationalist politics. Against those 'Pharisees' arguing that humanity had left behind the phase of national political claims, Fanon maintained that in the colonial and post-colonial countries 'the national period' had not even begun.[38]

By 1975, however, a decidedly different mood was apparent within ANC circles. In that year, as Angola became independent (with a self-professed Marxist-Leninist government coming to power and Cuban troops arriving to help it repel the invading South African army), an ANC strategy and tactics document associated the organization with 'the world's progressive forces' and looked toward the building of 'a nonracial, ultimately non-national world society; a society without class.'[39] Like the early optimism of the French Revolution, for a moment the South African vision of liberation overflowed the boundaries of the nation-state. We can recognize, here, a way in which the political ideals of equality and popular sovereignty contain a logic driving naturally toward the transnational. If universal equality is to be the central principle of law and government within the nation-state, on what grounds could a hierarchy of nations be legitimate?

The ANC's ascent to power in 1994 was clearly a victory for popular sovereignty. Yet, rather than flowing outward, the ANC's political vision seemed to contract in the wake of its victory over apartheid. One indication of this tendency was the reaction of South African government officials to the 1999 protests in Seattle, London, and Prague against the World Trade Organization, the IMF, and the World Bank. Where once the ANC surely would have aligned itself with 'the world's progressive forces' in calling for the cancellation of Third World debt and the protection of workers' rights, Finance Minister Trevor Manuel had only derision for the protestors who were, in his words, 'posing as television stars.'[40] If, twenty years earlier, the ANC had depended for its very survival upon a type of transnational solidarity (if not a fully fledged form of organizational internationalism) and had called upon youthful protestors in Europe and the United States to disrupt business as usual with the apartheid state, it now poured scorn on those who would once have been its allies. Internationalism might lie moldering in its grave, but global capitalism, Deputy President Thabo Mbeki declared, was inevitable and should not be resisted.[41]

Internationalism as ideology

In *The German Ideology*, Marx and Engels suggest that political belief is powerfully conditioned by material circumstances. But if this is the case, how can it be that contemporary social egalitarian internationalism appears relatively weak, while the globalization of capitalism has never been so intense and extensive?

Part of the answer lies in the fact that the term 'globalization' really encompasses two related processes with radically different effects. On the one hand, a set of technological transformations has broadened the range and increased the speed of transnational connections. This has occurred both in the areas of media and communications and (with a corresponding set of changes in trade and finance legislation both globally and nationally) in the mobility of financial capital. On the other hand, what this transformation has set in motion is not so much a new set of connections between nations as a reinvigorated field for national competition. Certainly, for the second-tier industrial countries – those hungriest for the manna of foreign investment – globalization means, first and foremost, a competition to create the cheapest labor market and so attract foreign investors to their shores. But while the race to become 'globally competitive' explains something about the behavior of contemporary states, it does not take us very far into the wider effects this process may have on contemporary forms of ideology. The protests in Seattle, London, and Prague, for example, suggest that both the images and the direct economic impacts of global capitalism are capable of stimulating a political response. The question to be asked, however, is how deep this form of egalitarian internationalism will run.

A preliminary answer might be found in the contrast between the collapse of the Second International and the organization of the International Brigades. What the experience of the Brigades demonstrates is that powerful, durable ideologies do not arise from the coincidental sharing of ideals. The Second International collapsed in the face of World War I because its structures and institutions were ultimately national. Its internationalism consisted of fraternal relations between national movements. By contrast, despite the fact that the Comintern was steadily steered away from its founding vision by Stalin, its existence as a genuinely transnational political institution provided the foundation for an internationalist form of political practice. Through such practice the otherwise hopelessly utopian vision of internationalism could appear not only plausible, but real.

To say that ideology takes firm root only through institutions and practices would seem to echo *The German Ideology*'s materialism, which, famously, 'does not explain practice from the idea but explains the formation of ideas from material practice [...]'[42] Yet where this model of ideology has always become troublesome is in its apparently mechanical rigidity. How, it has frequently been asked, could political actors go about the task of revolutionizing their institutions and practices when their mental faculties had already been conditioned by the institutions and practices of the past?

The solution to this chicken-and-egg problem is contained in the same text, though all too often it has been overlooked. If a bourgeois world produced only bourgeois ideas, the political project of proletarian revolution would be, quite literally, unthinkable. For Marx and Engels, this was clearly not the case. 'The existence of revolutionary ideas in a particular period,' they wrote, 'presupposes the existence of a revolutionary class.'[43] Thus, just as capitalism would produce its living, material contradiction in the form of the proletariat, the existence of that contradiction would provide the ground in which contradictory ideas could take root.

We should not read this argument too simplistically. There is no suggestion here that material conditions supply their own interpretation or that each and every worker would be inculcated with the revolutionary spirit simply by going to his or her job in the morning. What Marx and Engels suggest is that under certain material conditions, certain ideas become thinkable. Both the justice and the injustice of the factory regime can be conceived of by people for whom factory production is a common feature of life. Neither a justification of nor an attack on caste-stratified cattle-lending systems would be likely to have much resonance among computer programmers in Silicon Valley.

One of the ways, then, in which material conditions function ideologically is in making possible certain types of action. This is the process that Louis Althusser and Goran Therborn describe as 'ideological interpellation.'[44] Ideologies, in this sense, tell us what exists, what is right, what can be done, and what cannot.[45] Thus, both broad social conditions and the more particular structures of institutions might be thought of as acting ideologically. In this respect, internationalism has much in common with nationalism. Both are, to adopt Benedict Anderson's language, imagined communities of persons who, for the most part, will never meet one another.

One of Anderson's examples of this imagining in action is the mass ritual of reading the daily newspaper. Through the simultaneous performance of a common action, a tremendous number of disparate persons are linked to a common world.[46] Yet their connection to a specifically national world cannot be due to the simultaneity or even the commonality of the action. The *New York Times*, after all, features stories not only about New York City, but about Moscow, Rio de Janeiro, and Harare. Why, then, would a reader of the *Times* imagine him- or herself as American rather than Russian, Brazilian, or Zimbabwean? The answer, surely, is that the stories in the *New York Times* anchor themselves in a specifically American center, from which an outside world is observed. Deployments and shadings of language and discourse encourage the reader to find him- or herself situated in that perspectival center and to view the world through its lens.

Nothing about this suggests that only nation-states might be able to act as such lenses. In 1936, a reader of the *New York Times* might have found him- or herself connected, through its stories and language, to other Americans as an American. Yet, in the same time and place, the reader of a Communist Party newspaper would have been linked, through the same mechanisms of collective imagining, to political activists and workers throughout the world. The newspaper, in this case, is the ideological node at which a common identity is imagined, but the preconditions of that imagining go much farther: from the existence of a press and channels of distribution, to a whole variety of supporting institutions capable of legitimizing and reinforcing a particular newspaper's perspective or discourse.

In these things, the nation-state would seem to have clear advantages over any form of internationalism. The institutions and practices of the nation continue to loom large in everyday life. But there is nothing in the thought of the nineteenth- and twentieth-century social egalitarians to suggest that national and transnational political practices should be understood as mutually exclusive. Marx clearly did not believe that the proletariat would be able to think its way around the nationally rooted institutions of capitalism simply by adopting an internationalist political identity, though neither did he believe that a social revolution limited to the boundaries of the nation-state would be a meaningful one. The powers holding sway within the nation-state would have to be dealt with, but they would also have to be transcended. What we can now add is that it is in the beginnings of that transcendence, in the building of transnational political institutions, that internationalism as ideology could become living and real.

We can conclude from this that what has been referred to as globalization will not automatically result in the formation of new, transnational political identities. Instead, by easing the mobility of capital, the process currently under way has reinvigorated the notion of national competition, although today that competition is for investment rather than empire. To this extent, national and sub-national emancipatory projects are likely to become less meaningful, though no less attractive. As economic forces become increasingly able to slip out from under the nation-state, national democracies will find themselves with diminishing control over the material conditions of everyday life. Ordinary people, the ones most likely to find themselves adrift in the waves of global economic turbulence, will seek solace for their losses. They will seek control over the seemingly uncontrollable in national and cultural identity. But they will not find it there. The national and the cultural are concerned with matters of soul and conscience and homeland, and money has already declared its freedom from these.

SIX

The privation state

In 1950, when T. H. Marshall proposed that the highly developed countries were gradually but steadily working their way toward the achievement of social rights for their citizens, he did not foresee the sweeping counter-attack that Western capitalists and their political allies would eventually launch against this movement. By the 1980s, what the US constitution declared to be government's central purpose – the general welfare – had become a dirty term and a period of unbridled capitalist hubris was under way.

In the USA, the institutions devoted to social rights had always been minimal compared with those in continental Europe. Yet even the minimal 'welfare state' that existed in the USA came under attack in the 1980s. The truly decisive turn came in 1996 with the elimination of what had been the primary form of income support for families in poverty, Aid to Families with Dependent Children (AFDC), and its replacement by the Personal Responsibility and Work Opportunity Reconciliation Act (PRA).

In total, the PRA amounted to a dense condensation of culturally conservative and market-oriented policy objectives, from the privatization of social services to the demonization of out-of-wedlock births. Two of its elements were central to the new neoliberal vision. First, the notion of a federally guaranteed minimum income for those in poverty was sharply curtailed. While state governments were required by the Act to develop programs to replace AFDC, the PRA contained no guarantee that a person falling below the poverty line would receive support. Further, regardless of their circumstances, those persons who did receive income support would now be limited to five cumulative years of assistance. Second, the role of work requirements – previously a minor component of poverty alleviation programs – was massively expanded. The new state-level programs were mandated by the Act to require anyone receiving assistance to be working after no more than two years.[1]

The results of the new policy were swift and dramatic: a 44 percent drop in the number of welfare recipients within two years of the PRA's passage into law.[2] Of course, those now being shed from the welfare rolls did not necessarily find themselves employed in good jobs, earning decent wages. One early study found that of 137 Iowa families dropped from AFDC, 40 percent saw their monthly income rise by an average of $496. Forty-nine percent, though, lost an average of $384 per month.[3] A later study of former welfare recipients now making their way on to the job market revealed that most had no health insurance and many reported that they were often unable to pay rent and utility bills and sometimes skipped meals at the end of a month when the money ran out.[4] While the PRA demanded in strident and moralizing tones that the poor be made to work, it was curiously silent on the question of whether everyone who wanted to work could find a job, or whether the income earned at a minimum-wage position would be enough to bring an individual or a family above the poverty line.

Whether or not welfare reform could be considered a success, of course, depended on the definition of its objectives. Had the elimination or alleviation of poverty been marked out as its goal, the PRA's record would be a questionable one, at best. In 1998, just under 13 percent of the population lived below the poverty level – a 1 percent reduction from the number in 1995.[5] Taking into account the sustained economic expansion that occurred during the latter half of the 1990s, such a minor fluctuation could hardly be trumpeted as a major victory in the war against want. But such news was unlikely to trouble the members of Congress who drafted the new policy or the state-level administrators who oversaw its implementation.

In one sense, the new program repeatedly stressed the importance of work. Marking the shift in both policy and political valence, New York City's welfare offices, for example, were renamed 'Job Centers.' Yet whether or not people in need actually found jobs turned out to be of little or no importance. Instead, discouraging aid-seekers from applying for public assistance of any kind was openly pursued as a key element in the new approach to social services. As the newsletter of the Queens Job Center described their strategy: 'No matter how you phrase it, the goal of the Financial Planner, Employment Planner, Social Service Planner, and Resource Staff is the same: Redirect the participant to another source other than Temporary Assistance.'[6]

Why was striking people from the welfare rolls now a more pressing goal than lifting them out of poverty? A crucial touchstone of the neoliberal political vision was the notion that those receiving government income support were not truly in need of such assistance, they had simply been allowed to become dependent upon it. As Representatives in the House argued during a debate over the PRA,

> [...] the original intent of the welfare system has been lost. What was intended to be a compassionate provision to help people has turned into a destructive and permanent fixture of dependency for many who are entrapped within it.[7]

> For five million families, the average length of stay on welfare is thirteen years. The Democrats have coated the social safety net with glue and millions of Americans are crying for help to become unstuck [...] it is these same Democrats who are standing in the doors of the Nation's ghettos, refusing to let people out.[8]

Social welfare benefits, the argument ran, did not alleviate poverty, they condemned people to it.

Some in the private sector were quick to pick up on the idea that the elimination of public benefits was itself a benefit. In several states, the distribution of what little temporary income support now remained was shifted from paper checks to electronic debit cards, provided by a handful of large financial houses. But like wayward bank customers sanctioned for using a rival company's automatic teller machine, welfare recipients making withdrawals using the cards were charged a transaction fee, deductible from their benefits and payable to the financial firms operating the system. One might be excused for thinking that to a single parent struggling to survive in New York City on $448 per month, a $2.35 fee for each purchase of food or withdrawal of cash would represent a loss rather than a gain. Citigroup, the largest provider of electronic benefits transfer (EBT) services, saw it differently. 'The most important benefit,' the company's representatives told government regulators, 'is that EBT allows low-income individuals a point of entry into the mainstream of electronic banking.'[9] The important matter was not how much a person had to spend on things like food or shelter each month, but that they were as fully removed as possible from the world of public social services and incorporated instead into the world of private industry, commerce, and the market.

It was, of course, the persistent failure of the market economy to provide jobs and incomes for all which once led to the building of public social welfare institutions. As cross-national studies of social welfare regimes have consistently demonstrated, the levels of pre-transfer poverty produced by advanced industrial societies are both high and unvarying. Before taxes are collected and government bene-fits distributed, the USA, Canada, the UK, Sweden, the Netherlands, France, Italy, and Australia all generate approximately the same levels of relative poverty – around 20 percent of their populations.[10] The dif-ferences in post-transfer poverty rates, however, are dramatic. Over a ten-year period (1985–94), post-transfer poverty rates drop to around 13 percent in the USA, 6 percent in Germany, and less than 1 percent in the Netherlands.[11] It might be said, then, that the existence and extent of poverty in advanced industrial societies is the result of a choice made by political authorities, economic elites, and middle-class electorates. Yet, for the architects of 'welfare reform' in the USA, the problem to be solved had less to do with collective political choices than with individual economic ones:

> Sadly, many of these people have chosen to make their living for themselves and their families without working by choosing to take AFDC, food stamps, and countless other programs which cost over $300 billion annually. This is wrong and unfair for them and taxpayers, and it must stop. What the Personal Responsibility Act aims to do is to require individuals to look to themselves and their families and not to Washington in order to become productive members of society.[12]

What, exactly, would it mean for the poor to 'look to themselves and their families' to make their living? New York mayor Rudolph Giuliani offered this advice: 'If you can't get a job, start a small business. Start a little candy store. Start a little newspaper stand. Start a lemonade stand.'[13]

In one sense, this sort of giddy market fundamentalism represented a dreamlike denial of reality. Candy stores require business licenses, inventories, display cases, cash registers, and – unless the proprietor is lucky enough to own a piece of prime commercial real estate – rented premises, entailing security deposits and favorable credit histories. Anyone eligible to receive government income assistance was highly unlikely to have ready access to any of these. Giuliani's prosaic lemon-ade stand – the one business venture possibly within reach of those now being ejected from the social welfare system – would be a bad bet to provide for anyone's needs in a city like New York. To expect that tens of thousands of highly profitable lemonade stands might lift the poor, the unemployed, and the homeless out of poverty was nothing short of sheer lunacy. In another sense, however, the mayor's feverish Horatio Alger fantasy contained a coldly sober assessment of what the neoliberal state now stood for.

Poverty reduction was clearly not one of the new state's goals, nor was ensuring that all adult members of society earned their living through work. Had work itself been the crucial issue at stake (as some, such as sociologist William Julius Wilson, suggested it should have been), the creation of large-scale public works projects on the model of the Depression-era Works Progress Administration would surely have been the order of the day. But while some states developed public 'workfare' programs, these were both small in scale and temporary in duration, being tied to the same five-year limits as other forms of assistance. As the US economy slid into recession in 2001, the first generation of post-welfare poor reached the end of their eligibility even for 'workfare' with dimming hopes of finding employment in the private sector. But employment, or the lack thereof, was of little concern to the neoliberal state. Instead, its attention was now focused on a type of self-purification; a purging of the social egalitarian elements that had crept into advanced capitalism over the course of the twentieth century. More than anything else, 'welfare reform' announced a return of the capitalist state to its liberal fundamentals.

The results of the neoliberal revolution have been strikingly clear. In the USA, the gap between a fabulously wealthy capitalist elite and everyone else widened spectacularly. Between 1979 and 2005, pre-tax incomes for the poorest households grew by just over 1 percent, while middle-tier incomes rose by less than 1 percent. During the same period, pre-tax incomes for the richest 1 percent of American households grew by 200 percent. Most tellingly with respect to the political backing for this sweeping redistribution of resources, post-tax incomes for the richest 1 percent of households grew by 228 percent.[14]

The rollback of government regulation over the worlds of business and finance quickly led to dangerous forms of economic instability. As the US financial industry was gradually deregulated, a vast menagerie of increasingly complex and potentially volatile financial instruments proliferated. Many of these new investment products were linked to the home mortgage market, creating strong incentives for loosely regulated brokers to seek out new customers for home loans. The proliferation of mortgages on deceptively easy terms fueled an unprecedented run-up in home prices. Correspondingly, as home prices rose – skyrocketing in many parts of the country – the ability of borrowers to pay became less and less important to banks and mortgage brokers. Provided that the underlying value of the property was strong, foreclosure might be a disaster for the borrower, but not for the lender.

Yet the fact that working-class incomes had been effectively flat since the late 1970s meant that the real estate boom was built on sand. Between 2001 and 2007, home equity borrowing more than doubled, reaching $1.1 trillion.[15] Credit card debt added another $962 billion.[16] By 2007, many US consumers were no longer able to keep up with their monthly payments and a flood of bankruptcies in the mortgage industry began. As Wall Street investment banks – the hubristic titans of the 1980s and 1990s boom years – collapsed, global stock markets plunged, and layoffs cut hundreds of thousands of workers adrift.

Former chairman of the Federal Reserve Alan Greenspan told legislators in the House of Representatives that he was 'in a state of shocked disbelief' at the failure of the market economy to self-correct.[17] If, in fact, this was an accurate description of his reaction to the crisis, it could only have been the product of willful ignorance. In 1848, Marx and Engels warned that capitalists could be likened to 'the sorcerer who could no longer control the unearthly powers he had summoned forth.'[18] Even at this relatively early juncture in the development of global capitalism, Marx and Engels had recognized and described its volatile, crisis-prone nature. The Great Depression of the 1930s confirmed their observations in the most painful and destructive way. By 2008, anyone who believed that unregulated markets would produce nothing other than stable, steady economic growth and good life opportunities for anyone who wanted them was simply ignorant of well-demonstrated facts.

Crisis and possibility

The financial crisis that began in 2007, in other words, should have come as no surprise to anyone familiar with the social egalitarian critique of capitalism. What did come as a surprise, however, was the sudden reappearance of the term 'socialism' in American political discourse. As Washington assumed partial control of collapsed banks and discussed public bailouts of failing auto manufacturers, newspaper columnists and TV news commentators began to ask whether what was under way was a transition to socialism – a ques-

tion that had seemed light-years from the US political agenda only
months before.

Historians and political scientists have long studied the question
of why the USA stands out among the highly developed industrial
countries for its lack of a vibrant socialist political tradition and a
viable socialist electoral party. Werner Sombart argued that American
prosperity left workers relatively contented and uninterested in a
socialist alternative to capitalism. Frederick Jackson Turner held that
the country's open frontier dampened class tensions and promoted
individuality over class solidarity. Louis Hartz suggested that it was
only the battle against aristocratic privilege which had produced
a socialist tradition in Europe. Lacking a feudal history, the USA
developed no socialist movement. Others proposed that racial and
ethnic divisions undermined the development of a politically cohesive
American working class. Some noted that socialist and communist
parties had formed in the USA, but were snuffed out by waves of
political repression in the 1920s and 1950s.[19] Whatever the explanation,
though, the fact remained that, for most Americans, 'socialism' was a
foreign word – a term evoking fear and derision, rather than a viable
alternative to the policy agenda that had led to economic catastrophe.

On the surface, of course, it was obvious that 'socialism' was not
on the agenda. The Democratic Party that assumed control of Congress and the White House in 2008 had no connection to a declared
socialist tradition. No significant political figure in Washington or
elsewhere in the USA called for full-scale nationalization of industry
or public economic planning. During all the talk of bailouts for industry, terms such as 'class struggle' and 'equality' escaped no one's lips.

At a slightly deeper level, however, the core values of the broad
social egalitarian tradition were indeed part of the discussion. To
the extent that what was under consideration was government's role
in coordinating and regulating economic life for the purpose of
promoting public wellbeing, the issues that matter most to socialists,
communists, and social democrats – the use of public resources to
promote equal freedom for all – were very much in play. Yet the range
of that discussion and the depth of the policy proposals it would
produce were severely limited by the organizational weakness of the
left in the USA and its lack of a clear, cohesive political vision. Most
telling was the match-up of slogans in the 2008 presidential election,
during which both major parties attempted to attract voters with the
promise of 'Change.'

The economic crisis was an opportunity for change. For years, finance, insurance, and real estate firms had been the largest and most influential donors to political parties and candidates. Now they were on the ropes, appearing before congressional committees to beg for public funds. No crisis, though, offers up its own ready-made solution; there are always multiple possibilities for change. An opportunity was clearly at hand to achieve progress toward social equality not seen in the USA since the New Deal era. But this would come about only to the extent that the values on which such a project might be founded were clearly held by citizens organized and mobilized so as to be politically effective.

The way forward toward social equality cannot come about simply through the generation and discussion of ideas. One of the most fundamental lessons revealed by the careful study of politics is that organizations are responsible for bringing about political change. We remember Rosa Parks and Martin Luther King, yet we would never have known their names had they not been connected to the organized political forces that made the Civil Rights movement what it was. It is equally true, though, that organizations must be brought together around and animated by ideas. To be effective, they must have clear, coherent values to guide their actions. Reflecting on those values, then, is far from a waste of time; it is an essential, recurring element in the life of a political movement. It is only one element, though, and should not be assumed to substitute for others of equal importance.

Conclusion

This book has been about the core values of social egalitarian political thought. If these ideas were matters of common sense or unanimous agreement, such analysis and explication would be unnecessary. But the field of political philosophy will never be so simple or uncontested as this. The concepts discussed here have been met by powerful challenges from both sides of the political spectrum, and it seems safe to say that today there are more popular ideological currents than those rooted in the belief in equality. Popularity, however, is not necessarily reflective of accuracy, usefulness, or sustainability.

Consider, for example, the postmodernist challenge to the materialist theory of history. Since the late 1970s, academic circles have been swept by the metatheoretical view of history as fundamentally textual in nature: random, limitless, and free-floating – driven only by interpretation and reinterpretation from an infinite number of different perspectives. The natural political extension of this idea has been a celebration of agonistic self-expression: the politics of cultural identity. Yet the assertion of cultural identity has been powerless in the face of growing economic inequality, both within sovereign states and between them. Ethnic or racial pride cannot create the material basis for wellbeing and freedom when business owners choose to hoard their capital instead of creating jobs. Micro-national independence may be of questionable value when the highly interdependent global economy threatens to abandon people in isolated poverty. A theory of history that takes seriously the material constraints and possibilities of our world is better equipped than its competitors to explain the origins of inequality and the most effective strategies for combating it.

Something similar could be said with respect to the limitations of political theories proposing the expansion of liberty through either the elimination of government or its radical democratization. Anarchism offers the comfort of a puritanical position from which one's hands are never dirtied by political power, yet it also rejects the only mechanisms through which the power of privately amassed wealth might be matched. Political equality, the ideal at the heart of democratic theory, is a fundamental element of any genuinely egalitarian political philosophy. On its own, however, it is insufficient to guarantee the fullest expansion of equal freedom. Popular majorities and democratically elected governments are perfectly capable of promoting inegalitarian policies. The pursuit of genuine social equality requires democratic government, but it demands also that attention and action are constantly directed toward the economic foundations of social life.

The economic vision of social egalitarianism, however, has too often been reduced to a hopelessly inaccurate, though politically useful, caricature. The portrayal of socialism as either a flawless utopia or a nightmarish dystopia remains a common feature of political discourse on both the right and the left. For the right, the image of socialist totalitarianism serves as both a slippery slope and a straw target: any attempt at promoting material equality will inevitably lead to a total transformation of society resembling both Stalin's Russia and Orwell's *Nineteen Eighty-Four*. For the left, the insistence on socialism as a state of total perfection allows all responsibility for progress to be deferred pending a future revolution. All existing governments, actions, and policies can be ruthlessly criticized for leaving some human ill unaddressed, while the ideal of socialism as the answer to all problems remains unblemished.

What I hope to have demonstrated here is that the politics of equality are rooted not in utopian end-states, but in particular values. These values are in no way foreign to our everyday experience. They find expression in every public school, on every public sidewalk, and in every public park. They find expression in minimum wage laws and in environmental regulations. They are values that great movements of ordinary people have fought for in the past, but they are also values for the future. A world whose economic complexity and technological power put not only human wellbeing but human existence at risk cannot survive without them.

Notes

Introduction

1 Billy Wharton, 'Obama's no socialist. I should know,' *Washington Post*, 15 March 2009; 'What is socialism in 2009?,' *New York Times Online Edition*, http://roomfordebate.blogs.nytimes.com/2009/09/14/what-is-socialism-in-2009/.

2 T. H. Marshall, *Citizenship and Social Class, and Other Essays* (Cambridge: Cambridge University Press, 1950).

3 See, for example, Donald Sassoon, *One Hundred Years of Socialism: The West European Left in the Twentieth Century* (New York: New Press, 1996); Sheri Berman, *The Primacy of Politics: Social Democracy and the Making of Europe's Twentieth Century* (Cambridge: Cambridge University Press, 2006); Carl Boggs and David Plotke, *The Politics of Eurocommunism: Socialism in Transition* (Boston, MA: South End Press, 1999).

4 See Perry Anderson, *Considerations on Western Marxism* (London: NLB, 1976).

1 Historical materialism

1 Thomas Hobbes, *Leviathan*, ed. A. P. Martinich (Peterborough: Broadview Press, 2002).

2 Jean-Jacques Rousseau, *On the Social Contract*, in *The Basic Political Writings*, trans. and ed. Donald A. Cress (Indianapolis, IN: Hackett, 1987), p. 144.

3 Hobbes, pp. 94–5.

4 Ibid., pp. 126, 129.

5 Jean-Jacques Rousseau, *Discourse on the Origin of Inequality*, in *The Basic Political Writings*, trans. and ed. Donald A. Cress (Indianapolis, IN: Hackett, 1987), pp. 57, 65.

6 Rousseau, *On the Social Contract*, p. 170, n. 12.

7 John Locke, *Two Treatises of Government*, ed. Peter Laslett (Cambridge: Cambridge University Press, 1991), pp. 287–8. Locke's unique explanation of property rights has been traced to the newly transformed class position of English agrarian capitalists. Ellen Meiksins Wood, *The Origins of Capitalism* (New York: Monthly Review Press, 1999), pp. 88–9.

8 Adam Smith, *An Inquiry into the Nature and Causes of the Wealth of Nations* (Indianapolis, IN: Hackett, 1993), p. 10.

9 Rousseau, *Discourse on the Origin of Inequality*, p. 39.

10 Ibid., p. 40.

11 Ibid., p. 59.

12 Karl Marx, 'Preface to *A Critique of Political Economy*,' in *Karl Marx: Selected Writings*, ed. David McLellan (Oxford: Oxford University Press, 2000), p. 425.

13 Rousseau, *Discourse on the Origin of Inequality*, pp. 40–41.

14 Karl Marx and Friedrich Engels, *Manifesto of the Communist Party*, in *Later Political Writings*, ed. Terrell Carver (Cambridge:

Cambridge University Press, 1996), pp. 1–2.

15 G. A. Cohen, *Karl Marx's Theory of History: A Defence* (Princeton, NJ: Princeton University Press, 1978), p. 134.

16 Wood, p. 70; George C. Comninel, *Rethinking the French Revolution* (New York: Verso, 1987), pp. 166–7.

17 Duncan K. Foley, 'Recent developments in the labor theory of value,' *Review of Radical Political Economics*, 32(1) (2000): 1–39 (p. 6).

18 Jared Diamond, *Guns, Germs, and Steel* (New York: Norton, 1999).

19 Ibid., pp. 15, 19.

20 Ibid., p. 57.

21 Ibid., p. 88.

22 Ibid., pp. 88–90, 153–4, 168–9.

23 Ibid., pp. 268–9, 286–7.

24 Smith, p. 9.

25 Aristotle, *The Politics*, ed. Stephen Everson (Cambridge: Cambridge University Press, 1996), p. 13. See also Hobbes, pp. 127–8.

26 Cohen, p. 35.

27 Marx, 'Preface,' p. 425.

28 Ibid. G. A. Cohen argues that the 'economic structure' referred to in the 1859 Preface should be understood to mean the relations of production only, rather than the combination of forces and relations of production. Cohen, pp. 28–9.

29 Sarah Anderson et al., *Executive Excess 2007: The Staggering Social Cost of U.S. Business Leadership* (Washington, DC: Institute for Policy Studies, 2007), p. 5.

30 Rousseau, *On the Social Contract*, p. 143.

31 Cohen, p. 231.

32 Diamond, pp. 268–9.

33 Robert Tignor, 'Colonial chiefs in chiefless societies,' *Journal of Modern African Studies* 9(3) (1971): 341.

34 Cohen, p. 29.

35 Ellen Meiksins Wood, *Democracy against Capitalism: Renewing Historical Materialism* (Cambridge: Cambridge University Press, 1995), pp. 183–5.

36 Cohen, p. 158.

37 See, for example, Stanley Aronowitz, *The Politics of Identity: Class, Culture, Social Movements* (New York: Routledge, 1992); Kevin M. Cahill and Lene Johannessen, *Considering Class: Essays on the Discourse of the American Dream* (Berlin: LIT Verlag, 2007); Rosemary Crompton, *Class and Stratification: An Introduction to Current Debates* (Cambridge: Polity Press, 1993); Andre Gorz, *Farewell to the Working Class* (London: Pluto Press, 1982); Ralph Miliband, *Divided Societies: Class Struggle in Contemporary Capitalism* (Oxford: Clarendon Press, 1989); C. Wright Mills, *White Collar* (Oxford: Oxford University Press, 1956); Erik O. Wright, *Class Counts: Comparative Studies in Class Analysis* (Cambridge: Cambridge University Press, 1997).

38 Edward Bellamy, *Looking Backward* (New York: Penguin Books, 1986), p. 37.

39 Paul Taylor et al., *Inside the Middle Class: Bad Times Hit the Good Life* (Washington, DC: Pew Research Center, 2008), p. 8.

40 Diamond, pp. 268–9.

41 Cohen, p. 73; Leo Huberman and Paul M. Sweezy, *Introduction to Socialism* (New York: Monthly Review Press, 1968), p. 23.

42 US Bureau of Economic Analysis, *Corporate Profits: First Quarter 2008*, www.bea.gov/newsreleases/national/gdp/2008/gdp108f.htm.

43 Edward N. Wolff, 'Changes in household wealth in the 1980s and 1990s in the U.S.,' Working Paper 407, Levy Economics Institute of Bard College (2004), p. 30.

44 Plato, *The Republic*, trans. Raymond Larson (Arlington Heights, IL: Harlan Davidson, 1979), pp. 13–14.

45 Ibid., p. 86.

46 Aristotle, pp. 43, 71–2, 127–8.

47 Hobbes, pp. 94–6, 128–9, 138.

48 Locke, p. 350.

49 James Madison, 'Tenth Federalist Paper,' in Alexander Hamilton, James Madison, and John Jay, *The Federalist Papers* (New York: Bantam, 1982), p. 44.

50 Eduard Bernstein, *Evolutionary Socialism* (New York: Schocken Books, 1961), pp. 96, 101; Donald Sassoon, *One Hundred Years of Socialism: The West European Left in the Twentieth Century* (New York: New Press, 1996), p. 6; Sheri Berman, *The Primacy of Politics: Social Democracy and the Making of Europe's Twentieth Century* (Cambridge: Cambridge University Press, 2006), p. 21.

51 Sassoon, p. 10.

52 Erik Olin Wright, 'Compass points: towards a socialist alternative,' *New Left Review* 41 (2006): 103.

53 Stephen Jay Gould, *I Have Landed* (New York: Norton, 2002), p. 115.

54 Ibid., p. 244.

55 Diamond, p. 249.

56 Eric Hobsbawm, Introduction to Karl Marx, *Pre-Capitalist Economic Formations* (London: Lawrence & Wishart, 1964), pp. 19–20.

57 A detailed analysis of this history can be found in Mike Davis, *Prisoners of the American Dream* (New York: Verso, 1986).

58 See, for example, Terry Eagleton, *Marxism and Literary Criticism* (London: Routledge, 2002).

2 Equal freedom

1 Noberto Bobbio, *Left and Right* (Cambridge: Polity Press, 1996), p. 60. We should add that this line of demarcation is always drawn along local and provisional coordinates. When we pull back the lens to take in the broad sweep of the history of political thought, it becomes a moving target. Although the terminology is of more modern origin, it is probably not unreasonable for us to think of ancient Athenian democrats as representing the political left to their aristocratic opponents' right. In a similar sense, Gerrard Winstanley and the Diggers might be said to have represented the English left of the middle 1600s, arguing for common ownership of land against both the remnants of the feudal nobility and the nascent capitalist agrarian elite. But the ancient Athenian and the seventeenth-century communitarian did not share precisely the same understanding of what it meant to live in a society of equals.

2 Here, then, is an example of historical materialism's dual aspects. On the one hand, the materialist theory of history would seek to

explain the ways in which political philosophy is shaped and influenced by a society's relations of production. On the other hand, historical materialism would also recognize a space of possibility in which competing forms of political philosophy might argue for the virtues of differing potential relations of production.

3 Stuart White, *Equality* (Cambridge: Polity Press, 2007), pp. 14, 16.

4 Joseph Raz, *The Morality of Freedom* (Oxford: Oxford University Press, 1986), p. 235.

5 Steven Lukes, 'Socialism and equality,' in *The Socialist Idea: A Reappraisal*, ed. Leszek Kolakowski and Stuart Hampshire (London: Weidenfeld & Nicolson, 1974), p. 75.

6 Josiah Ober, *Mass and Elite in Democratic Athens: Rhetoric, Ideology, and the Power of the People* (Princeton, NJ: Princeton University Press, 1989), p. 57.

7 J. P. Mayer, 'Reflections on equality,' in *The Socialist Idea: A Reappraisal*, ed. Leszek Kolakowski and Stuart Hampshire (London: Weidenfeld & Nicolson, 1974), p. 60.

8 Ober, p. 7.

9 Marcus Tulius Cicero, *The Republic*, trans. Niall Rudd (Oxford: Oxford University Press 1998), pp. 30–31, 58.

10 Hobbes, pp. 93, 128–9.

11 Ibid., pp. 140–44.

12 Use of the term 'liberal' in contemporary American political discourse has diverged so far from its origins in the history of political thought that a clarification is probably necessary. Classical liberals (e.g. Locke, Smith, John Stuart Mill) view human beings as abstract individuals having natural rights to self-rule and the ownership of private property. Capitalism, with as little government interference as possible, is their preferred form of economic organization. Those referred to as liberals in contemporary American political discourse usually agree with the classical liberals that individuals should have rights to privacy and free speech, but sometimes disagree with the classical liberal contention that rights to private property are sacrosanct. Curiously, those now referred to in contemporary American discourse as 'conservatives' typically hold the economic ideals of classical liberals, though some (like classical conservatives) would prefer to see individual rights restrained within the boundaries of traditional, usually religious, norms.

13 Thomas More, *Utopia*, ed. Paul Turner (New York: Penguin Books, 2003), p. 25.

14 Ibid., pp. 53, 55.

15 Ibid., p. 110.

16 Gerrard Winstanley, *The Law of Freedom and Other Writings*, ed. Christopher Hill (Cambridge: Cambridge University Press, 2006).

17 See, among other studies, E. J. Hobsbawm, *Industry and Empire* (New York: Penguin Books, 1999).

18 Charles Fourier, *The Theory of the Four Movements*, ed. Gareth Stedman Jones and Ian Patterson (Cambridge: Cambridge University Press, 1996).

19 Leonardo Benevolo, *The Origins of Modern Town Planning* (Cambridge, MA: MIT Press, 1971), pp. 49–50.

20 Bellamy, pp. 65–6.

21 Benevolo, p. 51. More's Utopians have not entirely eliminated social misbehavior. Criminals on Utopia are enslaved, restrained with golden chains. More, pp. 67–8, 82, 85.

22 Milton Friedman, *Capitalism and Freedom* (Chicago, IL: University of Chicago Press, 1962), pp. 1–2.

23 G. A. Cohen, *Self-Ownership, Freedom, and Equality* (Cambridge: Cambridge University Press, 1995), pp. 67–8.

24 Isaiah Berlin, 'Two concepts of liberty,' in Robert E. Gooding and Philip Pettit (eds), *Contemporary Political Philosophy* (Oxford: Blackwell, 1997).

25 Friedman, p. 12.

26 Smith, p. 13.

27 More, p. 53.

28 'The only part of the conduct of anyone for which he is amenable to society is that which concerns others.' John Stuart Mill, *On Liberty* (Indianapolis, IN: Hackett, 1978), p. 9.

29 Robert Nozick, *Anarchy, the State, and Utopia* (New York: Basic Books, 1974), p. 151.

30 Ibid., pp. 161–2.

31 Smith, p. 11.

32 Ibid., p. 130.

33 Rousseau, *Discourse on the Origin of Inequality*, p. 55.

34 Ibid., pp. 67–8.

35 Rousseau, *On the Social Contract*, pp. 153–4, 160–62.

36 Ibid., p. 170, n. 12.

37 See, for example, William Godwin, *An Enquiry Concerning Political Justice* (Oxford: Oxford University Press, 1971); Pierre-Joseph Proudhon, *What Is Property?*, ed. Donald R. Kelley and Bonnie G. Smith (Cambridge: Cambridge University Press, 1994); Peter Kropotkin, *Mutual Aid: A Factor of Evolution* (Gloucester: Dodo Press 2007); Emma Goldman, *Anarchism and Other Essays* (Mineola, NY: Dover Publications, 1969).

38 During the middle 1800s, several experimental communities influenced by Owen and Fourier's designs were established in the USA: New Harmony (1825–29), Brook Farm (1841–47), the North American Phalanx (1841–56), La Reunion (1855–60). Anarchist communes have existed intermittently on rural farms and in temporarily unclaimed apartment buildings in cities such as New York, Berlin, and Copenhagen.

39 Norman Geras, 'Socialist hope in an age of catastrophe,' in Leo Panitch (ed.), *Socialist Register 1996* (London: Merlin Press, 1996), p. 243.

40 Karl Marx, *Economic and Philosophical Manuscripts*, in *Early Writings*, trans. Rodney Livingstone and Gregor Benton (New York: Vintage Books, 1975), p. 329.

41 Charles Fourier, *Dogmas and Dreams*, p. 215.

42 Marx, *Economic and Philosophical Manuscripts*, p. 326.

43 Larry M. Preston, 'Freedom, markets, and voluntary exchange,' *American Political Science Review*, 78(4) (1984): 959–70 (p. 961).

44 Jeremy Waldron, 'Homelessness and the issue of freedom,' in Robert E. Gooding and Philip Pettit (eds), *Contemporary Political Philosophy* (Oxford: Blackwell, 1997), p. 446.

45 Preston, pp. 961, 963.

46 Franklin D. Roosevelt,

'Message to the Congress on the State of the Union,' 11 January 1944, www.feri.org/archives/speeches/jan1144.cfm.

47 Friedman, pp. 16–17.

48 Marx and Engels, p. 20.

49 Swedish socialist leader Nils Karleby, quoted in Timothy Tilton, *The Political Theory of Swedish Social Democracy* (Oxford: Clarendon Press, 1990), p. 73.

50 Socialist International, *Declaration of Principles*, www.socialistinternational.org/4Principles/dofpeng2.html.

51 Cohen, *Self-Ownership*, pp. 122–3, 137.

3 Economy and society

1 Friedman, p. 13.

2 Ibid.

3 Preston, pp. 966–7.

4 Allen Ginsberg, 'America,' in *Howl and Other Poems* (San Francisco, CA: City Lights Books, 1985), p. 39.

5 Friedrich Engels, *Socialism: Utopian and Scientific* (New York: International Publishers, 1998), p. 35.

6 Alan Wertheimer, *Exploitation* (Princeton, NJ: Princeton University Press, 1996), p. 10.

7 Friedman, p. 15.

8 Karl Marx, *Capital*, vol. I, trans. Ben Fowkes (New York: Vintage Books, 1977), p. 266.

9 James Devine, 'Taxation without representation: reconstructing Marx's theory of capitalist exploitation,' in William Dugger (ed.), *Inequality: Radical Institutionalist Views on Race, Gender, Class, and Nation* (Westport, CT: Greenwood, 1996), p. 68.

10 Marx, *Capital*, vol. I, pp. 307, 312, 324–5.

11 See, for example, Paul A. Samuelson, 'Understanding the Marxian notion of exploitation: a summary of the so-called transformation problem between Marxian values and competitive prices,' *Journal of Economic Literature*, 9(2) (1971): 399–431; Ben Fine, *The Value Dimension: Marx versus Ricardo and Sraffa* (London: Routledge, 1986); David Laibman, 'Value and the quest for the core of capitalism,' *Review of Radical Political Economics*, 34 (2002): 159–78.

12 Foley, p. 21.

13 Duncan K. Foley, *Adam's Fallacy: A Guide to Economic Theology* (Cambridge: Belknap Press, 2006), p. 109.

14 US Census Bureau, *Statistical Abstract of the United States*, 2008, Table 623: 'Average hourly and weekly earnings 1990 to 2006,' www.census.gov/compendia/statab/cats/labor_force_employment_earnings/compensation_wages_and_earnings.html.

15 Milan Zafirovski, 'Measuring and making sense of labor exploitation in contemporary society: a comparative analysis,' *Review of Radical Political Economics*, 35 (2003): 469–70.

16 Hobbes, p. 158.

17 Locke, p. 289.

18 Smith, p. 12.

19 Ibid., p. 32.

20 In the USA, over half of all new small businesses close after four years. Amy E. Knaup, 'Survival and longevity in the business employment dynamics database,' *Monthly Labor Review*, 128(5) (2005): 50–56.

21 G. A. Cohen, 'The structure of proletarian unfreedom,' in John Roemer (ed.), *Analytical Marxism: Studies in Marxism and Social Theory* (Cambridge: Cambridge University Press, 1986).

22 Wertheimer, pp. 46–7, 49.

23 Economist Robin Hahnel has demonstrated this dynamic using a rational choice model of economic behavior. Robin Hahnel, *The ABCs of Political Economy: A Modern Approach* (London: Pluto Press, 2002), pp. 50–54.

24 See Chapter 1, Figure 1.4.

25 William E. Connolly, 'A note on freedom under socialism,' *Political Theory*, 5(4) (1977): 463.

26 Karl Marx, 'Critique of the Gotha Program,' in *Later Political Writings*, ed. Terrell Carver (Cambridge: Cambridge University Press, 1996), pp. 211–12; Duncan K. Foley, *Understanding Capital: Marx's Economic Theory* (Cambridge: Harvard University Press, 1986), p. 40.

27 Marx and Engels, *Manifesto of the Communist Party*, p. 19.

28 Bellamy, pp. 65–6.

29 Engels, pp. 66–9.

30 Robin Blackburn, 'Capital and social Europe,' *New Left Review*, 34 (2005): 101–2; Sassoon, pp. 707–11.

31 More, pp. 51–2.

32 Michael Barratt Brown, *Models in Political Economy* (London: Penguin Books, 1984), pp. 199–201.

33 Marx and Engels, p. 6.

34 Michael Harrington, *Socialism* (New York: Saturday Review Press, 1970), pp. 29, 35.

35 Hahnel, p. 255.

36 Hillel Ticktin, 'The problem is market socialism,' in Bertell Ollman (ed.), *Market Socialism: The Debate among Socialists* (New York: Routledge, 1998), p. 69.

37 More, pp. 56, 65; Bellamy, pp. 69, 71.

38 Bellamy, p. 89.

39 C. A. R. Crosland, *The Future of Socialism* (New York: Macmillan, 1957), p. 70.

40 Marx, *Economic and Philosophical Manuscripts*, pp. 346–7.

41 Bernstein, p. 202.

42 Crosland, p. 216.

43 Engels, pp. 47–8.

44 Brown, pp. 196–7.

45 Friedman, p. 13.

46 David Schweikart, 'Criticism of Ticktin,' in Bertell Ollman (ed.), *Market Socialism: The Debate among Socialists* (London: Routledge, 1998), pp. 126–7; Alec Nove, *The Economics of Feasible Socialism Revisited* (New York: HarperCollins Academic, 1991), pp. 43–4; Gabriel Kolko, *After Socialism* (London: Routledge, 2006), pp. 94–9.

47 This, of course, was the ideal put forward by the International Workers of the World (IWW) during the first quarter of the twentieth century.

48 Socialist International, *Declaration of Principles*.

49 Sassoon, p. 448.

50 George Bernard Shaw, *The Intelligent Woman's Guide to Socialism and Capitalism* (New Brunswick, NJ: Transaction Books, 1984), p. 101.

51 Nove, p. 57.

52 Amartya Sen, *Choice, Welfare, and Measurement* (Cambridge, MA: Harvard University Press, 1997), pp. 357, 365, 368.

53 Gøsta Esping-Andersen, *The*

Three Worlds of Welfare Capitalism (Princeton, NJ: Princeton University Press, 1990), p. 27.

54 Marx, 'Critique of the Gotha Program,' p. 214.

55 Ibid., p. 215.

56 Norman Geras, 'The Controversy about Marx and Justice,' www.marxists.org/reference/subject/philosophy/works/us/geras.htm.

57 Stuart White, *Equality* (Cambridge: Polity Press, 2007), p. 87.

58 Economists routinely demonstrate this principle using rational choice models and game theory. See, for example, Hahnel, pp. 103–5.

59 Friedman, pp. 23–4.

60 Socialist International, *Declaration of Principles*.

61 More, pp. 56, 61–3, 70.

62 Bellamy, pp. 57, 98–9, 118.

63 Alexei Gutnov et al., *The Ideal Communist City*, trans. Renee Neu Watkins (New York: George Braziller, 1971).

64 James M. Mayo, 'The manifestation of politics in architectural practice,' *Journal of Architectural Education*, 50(2) (1996): 81.

65 Ibid.

66 Gutnov et al., p. 117.

67 Ibid., pp. 68–9.

68 Ibid., p. 69.

69 Ibid., p. 87.

70 Ibid., pp. 95–6.

71 Christopher Pierson, *The Modern State* (London: Routledge, 1996), p. 56.

72 Berman, pp. 28, 30.

73 Evelyne Huber and John D. Stephens, 'The social democratic welfare state,' in Andrew Glyn (ed.), *Social Democracy in Neoliberal Times* (Oxford: Oxford University Press, 2001), p. 277.

74 David Harvey, *A Brief History of Neoliberalism* (Oxford: Oxford University Press, 2005), pp. 15, 17.

75 T. H. Marshall, *Class, Citizenship, and Social Development* (Chicago, IL: University of Chicago Press, 1964), p. 70.

76 *New York Times*, 15 March 1980.

77 Fred Block, *The Vampire State* (New York: New Press, 1996), p. 87.

78 Alan Brinkley, 'Reagan's revenge,' *New York Times Magazine*, 19 June 1994, pp. 36–7.

79 Quoted in Theda Skocpol, *Boomerang* (New York: Norton, 1996), p. 138.

80 Fourier, *Dogmas and Dreams*, p. 215; Marx, *Economic and Philosophical Manuscripts*, pp. 326, 329.

81 Karl Marx, *Capital*, vol. 3, in Karl Marx and Friedrich Engels, *Collected Works*, vol. 37 (London: Lawrence & Wishart, 1998), pp. 806–8.

82 More, pp. 56–7, 73, 78–9.

83 Ibid., p. 56.

84 Marx, *Economic and Philosophical Manuscripts*, p. 361.

85 Pietro Basso, *Modern Times, Ancient Hours* (London: Verso, 2003), p. 100; US Census Bureau, *Statistical Abstract of the United States*, 2008, Table 583: 'Employed civilians and weekly hours: 1980 to 2006,' http://www.census.gov/compendia/statab/cats/labor_force_employment_earnings/employed_persons.html.

86 Cohen, *Karl Marx's Theory of History*, p. 318.

87 Cohen, *Self-Ownership, Freedom, and Equality*, pp. 54–5, 237.

88 More, pp. 64–5, 83–5.

89 Marx, *Economic and Philosophical Manuscripts*, p. 379.

90 Bellamy, p. 191.

91 Tilton, p. 52.

4 Democracy

1 Friedrich Nietzsche proposes a similar vision, though his connection to an anarchist or libertarian tradition is more contested than is Rand's.

2 Daniel Guérin, *Anarchism* (New York: Monthly Review Press, 1970), p. 12.

3 Hobbes, p. 95.

4 Ibid., pp. 98, 128–9.

5 Ibid., p. 162.

6 Robert Paul Wolff, *In Defense of Anarchism* (New York: Harper & Row, 1970), p. 4.

7 Pierre-Joseph Proudhon, *Idée générale de la révolution au XIXe siècle*, quoted in Guerin, pp. 15–16.

8 Paul Thomas, *Karl Marx and the Anarchists* (London: Routledge & Kegan Paul, 1980), pp. 188, 229–30; See also Marx, 'Critique of the Gotha Program,' pp. 213–15.

9 Emma Goldman, 'Anarchism: what it really stands for,' in Nancy S. Love (ed.), *Dogmas and Dreams* (CQ Press, 2006), p. 357.

10 Ibid., p. 359.

11 Mikhail Bakunin, 'Scientific anarchism,' in Nancy S. Love (ed.), *Dogmas and Dreams* (CQ Press, 2006), pp. 389, 393.

12 Robert Paul Wolff, pp. 12–13, 16.

13 Goldman, pp. 355–6.

14 Robert Paul Wolff, p. 18.

15 Peter Kropotkin, *Mutual Aid: A Factor of Evolution* (New York: New York University Press, 1972).

16 Bakunin, pp. 388–9.

17 Goldman, p. 358; Bakunin, p. 397.

18 Goldman, pp. 360–61.

19 See, for example, Pablo Fajnzylber, Daniel Lederman, and Norman Loayza, 'Inequality and violent crime,' *Journal of Law and Economics*, 45 (2002): 1–40.

20 Jeffrey H. Reiman, *In Defense of Political Philosophy* (New York: Harper & Row, 1972), p. 42.

21 Guérin, p. 46.

22 Ibid., p. 31.

23 Ibid.

24 Robert A. Dahl, *On Democracy* (New Haven, CT: Yale University Press, 1998), p. 10.

25 David Held, *Models of Democracy* (Stanford, CA: Stanford University Press, 2006), p. 18.

26 Ibid., pp. 98–9.

27 Mill, pp. 4, 109.

28 Wood, *The Origins of Capitalism*, p. 276.

29 Rousseau, *On the Social Contract*, p. 170, n. 12; see also Held, p. 59.

30 Karl Marx, *On the Jewish Question*, in *Early Writings*, trans. Rodney Livingstone and Gregor Benton (New York: Vintage Books, 1975), p. 219.

31 Dahl, pp. 85–6.

32 Thomas, p. 344.

33 See, for example, Friedman, p. 10.

34 Marx and Engels, p. 19.

35 Karl Marx and Friedrich Engels, *Collected Works* (New York: International Publishers, 1975), p. 227.

36 August H. Nimtz, Jr, *Marx and Engels: Their Contribution to the Democratic Breakthrough*

(Albany: State University of New York Press, 2000).

37 Sassoon, p. 24.

38 Ibid., p. 10. In France, voting rights for working-class men were achieved as a result of the 1848 revolution. In Germany, manhood suffrage was achieved in 1871, largely as a result of the work of two smaller parties that would join forces in 1875 to form the German Social Democratic Party.

39 Adam Przeworski, *Capitalism and Social Democracy* (Cambridge: Cambridge University Press, 1985), p. 42; Claus Offe and Volker Runge, 'Theses on the theory of the state,' *New German Critique*, 6 (1975): 140.

40 Przeworski, p. 43.

41 Karl Marx, 'The civil war in France,' in *Later Political Writings*, ed. Terrell Carver (Cambridge: Cambridge University Press, 1996), p. 181.

42 Ober, p. 76.

43 Ibid., pp. 80–81.

44 Rousseau, *On the Social Contract*, p. 141.

45 Ibid., pp. 142–3, 148.

46 Ibid., p. 203.

47 Ibid., p. 198.

48 Marx, 'The civil war in France,' pp. 184–5.

49 Ibid., p. 187.

50 See, for example, V. I. Lenin, 'Report on the Unity Congress of the R.S.D.L.P.,' www.marxists.org/ archive/lenin/works/1906/rucong/viii. htm.

51 V. I. Lenin, *State and Revolution* (New York: International Publishers, 1943), pp. 43–4.

5 Internationalism

1 US Census Bureau, 'U.S. international trade in goods and services,' www.census.gov/foreign-trade/ Press-Release/2007pr/final_revisions/ exh1.txt.

2 Johann Gottfried von Herder, 'Essay on the origin of language,' in F. M. Barnard (ed. and trans.), *J. G. Herder on Social and Political Culture* (Cambridge: Cambridge University Press, 1969), p. 168.

3 Doug Henwood, *Wall Street* (London: Verso, 1997), p. 113.

4 Perry Anderson, *Considerations on Western Marxism* (London: NLB, 1976), p. 121.

5 Benedict Anderson, *Imagined Communities* (London: Verso, 1983), p. 11.

6 Eric Hobsbawm, *The Age of Capital: 1848–1875* (London: Abacus, 1997), p. 105.

7 Ibid., pp. 107–8.

8 Karl Marx, *Critical Notes on 'The King of Prussia and Social Reform'*, in *Early Writings*, trans. Rodney Livingstone and Gregor Benton (New York: Vintage Books, 1975), p. 415.

9 Marx and Engels, *Manifesto of the Communist Party*, p. 13.

10 Ibid., p. 17.

11 Roman Szporluk, *Communism and Nationalism* (New York: Oxford University Press, 1988), p. 35.

12 Karl Marx and Friedrich Engels, *The Holy Family*, in Karl Marx, *On Revolution*, ed. Saul K. Padover (New York: McGraw-Hill, 1971), p. 23.

13 Paul Thomas, *Alien Politics* (New York: Routledge, 1994), p. 84.

14 Solomon F. Bloom, *The World*

of Nations (New York: AMS Press, 1967), p. 38.

15 Karl Marx and Friedrich Engels, *The German Ideology* (New York: International Publishers, 1995), p. 55.

16 Karl Marx, 'The class struggles in France, 1848–50,' in Karl Marx, *On Revolution*, ed. Saul K. Padover (New York: McGraw-Hill, 1971), p. 162.

17 Karl Marx, 'The revolutionary movement,' in Karl Marx, *On Revolution*, ed. Saul K. Padover (New York: McGraw-Hill, 1971), p. 44.

18 Marx and Engels, *Manifesto of the Communist Party*, pp. 4–5.

19 Marx, 'Critique of the Gotha Program,' pp. 217–18.

20 Reproduced in John Riddell (ed.), *Lenin's Struggle for a Revolutionary International* (New York: Monad Press, 1986), pp. 24–5.

21 Ibid., pp. 26–7.

22 Ibid., p. 146.

23 Ibid., p. 187.

24 Marcel Liebman, *Leninism under Lenin* (London: Merlin Press, 1975), p. 361.

25 Ibid., p. 408.

26 Jane Degras (ed.), *The Communist International 1919–1943 Documents* (London: Frank Cass & Co., 1971), p. 16.

27 See, for example, Gilles Perrault, *The Red Orchestra* (New York: Simon & Schuster, 1969).

28 E. H. Carr, *The Comintern and the Spanish Civil War* (London: Macmillan, 1984), p. 15.

29 Verle B. Johnston, *Legions of Babel* (University Park: Pennsylvania State University Press, 1967), p. 36.

30 Peter N. Carroll, *The Odyssey of the Abraham Lincoln Brigade* (Stanford, CA: Stanford University Press, 1994), pp. 9–10.

31 Johnston, p. 151.

32 Carroll, pp. 71–2.

33 Ibid., pp. 66–7; Alvah Bessie and Albert Prago (eds), *Our Fight* (New York: Monthly Review Press, 1987), pp. 66, 69–70.

34 Carroll, pp. 15–16.

35 Ibid., p. 71.

36 Vladimir Shubin, *ANC: A View from Moscow* (Bellville: Mayibuye Books, 1999), p. 41.

37 Quoted in Tom Lodge, *Black Politics in South Africa since 1945* (Johannesburg: Ravan Press, 1983), p. 302.

38 Frantz Fanon, *The Wretched of the Earth* (New York: Grove Press, 1968), pp. 246–7.

39 African National Congress, *Forward to Freedom* (1975), www.anc.org.za/ancdocs/history/forwd75.html.

40 Republic of South Africa: Ministry of Finance, 'Budget speech by Trevor A. Manuel' (23 February 2000), p. 2.

41 Republic of South Africa: Communication Service, 'Report on the visit of Executive Deputy President T. M. Mbeki to Davos, Switzerland' (2 February 1997), p. 1.

42 Marx and Engels, *The German Ideology*, p. 58.

43 Ibid., p. 65.

44 Louis Althusser, *Lenin and Philosophy* (New York: Monthly Review Press, 1971); Goran Therborn, *The Ideology of Power and the Power of Ideology* (London: Verso, 1980).

45 Therborn, p. 18.

46 Benedict Anderson, *Imagined Communities*, pp. 35–6.

6 The privation state

1 US: Personal Responsibility and Work Opportunity Reconciliation Act of 1996 (P.L. 104-193).

2 US Department of Health and Human Services – Administration for Children and Families, *Change in Welfare Caseloads*, January 1999, www.acf.dhhs.gov/news/stats/caseload.htm.

3 *New York Times*, 30 June 1997.

4 *Washington Post*, 3 August 1999.

5 US Census Bureau, *Statistical Abstract of the United States*, 2000, Table 759: 'Persons below poverty level by state: 1980 to 1998', www.census.gov/prod/2001pubs/statab/sec14.pdf.

6 Quoted in Jason DeParle, 'What Welfare-to-Work really means,' *New York Times Magazine*, 20 December 1998, p. 55.

7 Rep. Bryant (TN), 'Modern welfare system has not worked,' *Congressional Record*, 141(54), H3717 (23 March 1995).

8 Rep. Pryce (OH), 'Help – I've fallen and I can't get up,' *Congressional Record*, 141(54), H3578 (23 March 1995).

9 *New York Times*, 16 August 1999.

10 Lane Kenworthy, 'Do social-welfare policies reduce poverty? A cross-national assessment,' Working Paper no. 188, Luxemburg Income Study (1998).

11 Robert E. Goodin, Bruce Headey, Ruud Muffels and Henk-Jan Dirven, *The Real Worlds of Welfare Capitalism* (Cambridge: Cambridge University Press, 1999), p. 276.

12 Rep. Bryant (TN), 'Modern welfare system has not worked,' H3717.

13 Quoted in DeParle, p. 89.

14 *Financial Times*, 7 April 2008.

15 *New York Times*, 27 March 2008.

16 Ibid., 13 July 2008.

17 Ibid., 24 October 2008.

18 Marx and Engels, *Manifesto of the Communist Party*, p. 6.

19 See Eric Foner, 'Why is there no socialism in the United States?,' *History Workshop*, 17 (1984).

Bibliography

African National Congress (1975) *Forward to Freedom*, www.anc. org.za/ancdocs/history/forwd75. htm.

Althusser, L. (1971) *Lenin and Philosophy*, New York: Monthly Review Press.

Anderson, B. (1983) *Imagined Communities*, London: Verso.

Anderson, P. (1976) *Considerations on Western Marxism*, London: NLB.

Anderson, S. et al. (2007) *Executive Excess 2007: The Staggering Social Cost of US Business Leadership*, Washington, DC: Institute for Policy Studies.

Aristotle (1996) *The Politics*, ed. Stephen Everson, Cambridge: Cambridge University Press.

Aronowitz, S. (1992) *The Politics of Identity: Class, Culture, Social Movements*, New York: Routledge.

Bakunin, M. (2006) 'Scientific anarchism,' in N. S. Love (ed.), *Dogmas and Dreams*, Washington, DC: CQ Press.

Basso, P. (2003) *Modern Times, Ancient Hours*, London: Verso.

Bellamy, E. (1986) *Looking Backward*, New York: Penguin Books.

Benevolo, L. (1971) *The Origins of Modern Town Planning*, Cambridge, MA: MIT Press.

Berman, S. (2006) *The Primacy of Politics: Social Democracy and the Making of Europe's Twentieth Century*, Cambridge: Cambridge University Press.

Bernstein, E. (1961) *Evolutionary Socialism*, New York: Schocken Books.

Bessie, A. and A. Prago (1987) *Our Fight*, New York: Monthly Review Press.

Blackburn, R. (2005) 'Capital and social Europe,' *New Left Review*, 34.

Block, F. (1996) *The Vampire State*, New York: New Press.

Bloom, S. F. (1967) *The World of Nations*, New York: AMS Press.

Boggs, C. and D. Plotke (1999) *The Politics of Eurocommunism: Socialism in Transition*, Boston, MA: South End Press.

Brown, M. B. (1984) *Models in Political Economy*, London: Penguin Books.

Cahill, K. M. and L. Johannessen (eds) (2007) *Considering Class: Essays on the Discourse of the American Dream*, Berlin: LIT Verlag.

Carr, E. H. (1984) *The Comintern and the Spanish Civil War*, London: Macmillan.

Carroll, P. N. (1994) *The Odyssey of the Abraham Lincoln Brigade*, Stanford, CA: Stanford University Press.

Cicero, M. T. (1998) *The Republic*, trans. Niall Rudd, Oxford: Oxford University Press.

Cohen, G. A. (1986) 'The structure of proletarian unfreedom,' in J. Roemer (ed.), *Analytical Marxism: Studies in Marxism and Social Theory*, Cambridge: Cambridge University Press.

— (1978) *Karl Marx's Theory of History: A Defence*, Princeton, NJ: Princeton University Press.

— (1995) *Self-Ownership, Freedom, and Equality*, Cambridge: Cambridge University Press.

Comninel, G. C. (1987) *Rethinking the French Revolution*, New York: Verso.

Crompton, R. (1993) *Class and Stratification: An Introduction to Current Debates*, Cambridge: Polity Press.

Crosland, C. A. R. (1957) *The Future of Socialism*, New York: Macmillan.

Dahl, R. A. (1988) *On Democracy*, New Haven, CT: Yale University Press.

Davis, M. (1986) *Prisoners of the American Dream*, New York: Verso.

Degras, J. (1971) *The Communist International 1919–1943 Documents*, London: Frank Cass & Co.

DeParle, J. (1998) 'What Welfare-to-Work really means,' *New York Times Magazine*, 20 December.

Devine, J. (1996) 'Taxation without representation: reconstructing Marx's theory of capitalist exploitation,' in W. Dugger (ed.), *Inequality: Radical Institutionalist Views on Race, Gender, Class, and Nation*, Westport, CT: Greenwood.

Diamond, J. (1999) *Guns, Germs, and Steel*, New York: Norton.

Eagleton, T. (2002) *Marxism and Literary Criticism*, London: Routledge.

Engels, F. (1998) *Socialism: Utopian and Scientific*, New York: International Publishers.

Esping-Andersen, G. (1990) *The Three Worlds of Welfare Capitalism*, Princeton, NJ: Princeton University Press.

Fajnzylber, P., D. Lederman and N. Loayza (2002) 'Inequality and violent crime,' *Journal of Law and Economics*, 45.

Fine, B. (1986) *The Value Dimension: Marx versus Ricardo and Sraffa*, London: Routledge.

Foley, D. K. (1986) *Understanding Capital: Marx's Economic Theory*, Cambridge, MA: Harvard University Press.

— (2000) 'Recent developments in the labor theory of value,' *Review of Radical Political Economics*, 32(1).

— (2006) *Adam's Fallacy: A Guide to Economic Theology*, Cambridge: Belknap Press.

Foner, E. (1984) 'Why is there no socialism in the United States?,' *History Workshop*, 17.

Friedman, M. (1962) *Capitalism and Freedom*, Chicago, IL: University of Chicago Press.

Geras, N. (1996) 'Socialist hope in an age of catastrophe,' in L. Panitch (ed.), *Socialist Register 1996*, London: Merlin Press.

— (n.d.) 'The controversy about Marx and Justice,' www.marxists.org/reference/subject/philosophy/works/us/geras.htm.

Ginsberg, A. (1985) 'America,' in *Howl and Other Poems*, San Francisco, CA: City Lights Books.

Goldman, E. (2006) 'Anarchism: what it really stands for,' in N. S. Love (ed.), *Dogmas and Dreams*, Washington, DC: CQ Press.

Goodin, R. E., B. Headey, R. Muffels and H.-J. Dirven (1999) *The Real Worlds of Welfare Capitalism*, Cambridge: Cambridge University Press.

Gorz, A. (1982) *Farewell to the Working Class*, London: Pluto Press.

Gould, S. J. (2002) *I Have Landed*, New York: Norton.

Guérin, D. (1970) *Anarchism*, New York: Monthly Review Press.

Gutnov, A. et al. (1971) *The Ideal Communist City*, trans. Renee Neu Watkins, New York: George Braziller.

Hahnel, R. (2002) *The ABCs of Political Economy: A Modern Approach*, London: Pluto Press.

Harrington, M. (1970) *Socialism*, New York: Saturday Review Press.

Harvey, D. (2005) *A Brief History of Neoliberalism*, Oxford: Oxford University Press.

Held, D. (2006) *Models of Democracy*, Stanford, CA: Stanford University Press.

Henwood, D. (1997) *Wall Street*, London: Verso.

Herder, J. G. von (1969) 'Essay on the origin of language,' in F. M. Barnard (ed. and trans.), *J. G. Herder on Social and Political Culture*, Cambridge: Cambridge University Press.

Hobbes, T. (2002) *Leviathan*, ed. A. P. Martinich, Peterborough: Broadview Press.

Hobsbawm, E. J. (1964) Introduction to *Pre-Capitalist Economic Formations* by Karl Marx, London: Lawrence & Wishart.

— (1997) *The Age of Capital*, London: Abacus.

— (1999) *Industry and Empire*, New York: Penguin Books.

Huber, E. and J. D. Stephens (2001) 'The social democratic welfare state,' in A. Glyn (ed.), *Social Democracy in Neoliberal Times*, Oxford: Oxford University Press.

Huberman, L. and P. M. Sweezy (1968) *Introduction to Socialism*, New York: Monthly Review Press.

Johnston, V. B. (1967) *Legions of Babel*, University Park: Pennsylvania State University Press.

Kenworthy, L. (1998) 'Do social-welfare policies reduce poverty? A cross-national assessment,' Working Paper no. 188, Luxemburg Income Study.

Knaup, A. E. (2005) 'Survival and longevity in the Business Employment Dynamics Database,' *Monthly Labor Review*, 128(5).

Kolko, G. (2006) *After Socialism*, London: Routledge.

Kropotkin, P. (1972) *Mutual Aid: A Factor of Evolution*, New York: New York University Press.

Laibman, D. (2002) 'Value and the quest for the core of capitalism,' *Review of Radical Political Economics*, 34.

Lenin, V. I. (n.d.) 'Report on the Unity Congress of the R.S.D.L.P.,' www.marxists.org/archive/lenin/works/1906/rucong/viii.htm.

— (1943) *State and Revolution*, New York: International Publishers.

Liebman, M. (1975) *Leninism under Lenin*, London: Merlin Press.

Locke, J. (1991) *Two Treatises of Government*, ed. Peter Laslett,

Cambridge: Cambridge University Press.

Lodge, T. (1983) *Black Politics in South Africa since 1945*, Johannesburg: Ravan Press.

Madison, J. (1982) 'Tenth Federalist Paper,' in A. Hamilton, J. Madison and J. Jay, *The Federalist Papers*, New York: Bantam.

Marshall, T. H. (1950) *Citizenship and Social Class, and Other Essays*, Cambridge: Cambridge University Press.

Marx, K. (1971a) 'The class struggles in France, 1848–50,' in K. Marx, *On Revolution*, ed. S. K. Padover, New York: McGraw-Hill.

— (1971b) 'The revolutionary movement,' in Karl Marx, *On Revolution*, ed. S. K. Padover, New York: McGraw-Hill.

— (1975a) *Critical Notes on 'The King of Prussia and Social Reform'*, in *Early Writings*, trans. R. Livingstone and G. Benton, New York: Vintage Books.

— (1975b) *Economic and Philosophical Manuscripts*, in *Early Writings*, trans. R. Livingstone and G. Benton, New York: Vintage Books.

— (1977) *Capital*, vol. I, trans. B. Fowkes, New York: Vintage Books.

— (1996a) 'Critique of the Gotha Program,' in *Later Political Writings*, ed. T. Carver, Cambridge: Cambridge University Press.

— (1996b) 'The civil war in France,' in *Later Political Writings*, ed. T. Carver, Cambridge: Cambridge University Press.

— (1998) *Capital*, vol. 3, in K. Marx and F. Engels, *Collected Works*, vol. 37, London: Lawrence & Wishart.

— (2000) 'Preface to *A Critique of Political Economy*,' in *Karl Marx: Selected Writings*, ed. David McLellan, Oxford: Oxford University Press.

Marx, K. and F. Engels (1971) *The Holy Family*, in K. Marx, *On Revolution*, ed. S. K. Padover, New York: McGraw-Hill.

— (1975) *Collected Works*, New York: International Publishers.

— (1995) *The German Ideology*, New York: International Publishers.

— (1996) *Manifesto of the Communist Party*, in *Later Political Writings*, ed. Terrell Carver, Cambridge: Cambridge University Press.

Mayer, J. P. (1974) 'Reflections on equality,' in *The Socialist Idea: A Reappraisal*, ed. L. Kolakowski and S. Hampshire, London: Weidenfeld & Nicolson.

Mayo, J. M. (1996) 'The manifestation of politics in architectural practice,' *Journal of Architectural Education*, 50(2).

Miliband, R. (1989) *Divided Societies: Class Struggle in Contemporary Capitalism*, Oxford: Clarendon Press.

Mill, J. S. (1978) *On Liberty*, Indianapolis, IN: Hackett.

Mills, C. W. (1956) *White Collar*, Oxford: Oxford University Press.

More, T. (2003) *Utopia*, ed. P. Turner, New York: Penguin Books.

Nimtz, A. H., Jr. (2000) *Marx and Engels: Their Contribution to the Democratic Breakthrough*, Albany: State University of New York Press.

Nove, A. (1991) *The Economics of Feasible Socialism Revisited*, New York: HarperCollins Academic.

Nozick, R. (1974) *Anarchy, the State, and Utopia*, New York: Basic Books.

Ober, J. (1989) *Mass and Elite in Democratic Athens: Rhetoric, Ideology, and the Power of the People*, Princeton, NJ: Princeton University Press.

Offe, C. and V. Runge (1975) 'Theses on the theory of the state,' *New German Critique*, 6.

Perrault, G. (1969) *The Red Orchestra*, New York: Simon & Schuster.

Pierson, C. (1996) *The Modern State*, London: Routledge.

Plato (1979) *The Republic*, trans. R. Larson, Arlington Heights, IL: Harlan Davidson.

Preston, L. M. (1984) 'Freedom, markets, and voluntary exchange,' *American Political Science Review*, 78(4).

Przeworski, A. (1985) *Capitalism and Social Democracy*, Cambridge: Cambridge University Press.

Reiman, J. H. (1972) *In Defense of Political Philosophy*, New York: Harper & Row.

Rep. Bryant (TN) (1995) 'Modern welfare system has not worked,' *Congressional Record*, 141(54), H3717, 23 March.

Rep. Pryce (OH) (1995) 'Help – I've fallen and I can't get up,' *Congressional Record*, 141(54), H3578, 23 March.

Republic of South Africa (1997) Communication Service, 'Report on the visit of Executive Deputy President T. M. Mbeki to Davos, Switzerland,' 2 February.

— (2000) Ministry of Finance, 'Budget speech by Trevor A. Manuel,' 23 February.

Riddell, J. (1986) *Lenin's Struggle for a Revolutionary International*, New York: Monad Press.

Roosevelt, F. D. (1944) 'Message to the Congress on the State of the Union,' 11 January, www.feri.org/archives/speeches/jan1144.cfm.

Rousseau, J.-J. (1987a) *Discourse on the Origin of Inequality*, in *The Basic Political Writings*, trans. and ed. D. A. Cress, Indianapolis, IN: Hackett.

— (1987b) *On the Social Contract*, in *The Basic Political Writings*, trans. and ed. D. A. Cress, Indianapolis, IN: Hackett.

Samuelson, P. A. (1971) 'Understanding the Marxian notion of exploitation: a summary of the so-called transformation problem between Marxian values and competitive prices,' *Journal of Economic Literature*, 9(2).

Sassoon, D. (1996) *One Hundred Years of Socialism: The West European Left in the Twentieth Century*, New York: New Press.

Schweikart, D. (1998) 'Criticism of Ticktin,' in B. Ollman (ed.), *Market Socialism: The Debate among Socialists*, London: Routledge.

Sen, A. (1997) *Choice, Welfare, and Measurement*, Cambridge, MA: Harvard University Press.

Shaw, G. B. (1984) *The Intelligent Woman's Guide to Socialism and Capitalism*, New Brunswick, NJ: Transaction Books.

Shubin, V. (1999) *ANC: A View from Moscow*, Bellville: Mayibuye Books.

Skocpol, T. (1996) *Boomerang*, New York: Norton.

Smith, A. (1993) *An Inquiry into the Nature and Causes of the Wealth of Nations*, Indianapolis, IN: Hackett.

Socialist International (n.d.) *Declaration of Principles*, www.socialistinternational. org/4Principles/dofpeng2. html.

Szporluk, R. (1988) *Communism and Nationalism*, New York: Oxford University Press.

Taylor, P. et al. (2008) *Inside the Middle Class: Bad Times Hit the Good Life*, Washington, DC: Pew Research Center.

Therborn, G. (1980) *The Ideology of Power and the Power of Ideology*, London: Verso.

Thomas, P. (1980) *Karl Marx and the Anarchists*, London: Routledge & Kegan Paul.

— (1994) *Alien Politics*, New York: Routledge.

Ticktin, H. (1998) 'The problem is market socialism,' in B. Ollman (ed.), *Market Socialism: The Debate among Socialists*, New York: Routledge.

Tignor, R. (1971) 'Colonial chiefs in chiefless societies,' *Journal of Modern African Studies*, 9(3).

Tilton, T. (1990) *The Political Theory of Swedish Social Democracy*, Oxford: Clarendon Press.

US Bureau of Economic Analysis (n.d.) *Corporate Profits: First Quarter 2008*, www.bea.gov/ newsreleases/national/gdp/2008/ gdp108f.htm.

US Census Bureau (n.d.) 'U.S. international trade in goods and services,' www. census.gov/foreign-trade/Press-Release/2007pr/final_revisions/ exh1.txt.

— (2000) *Statistical Abstract of the United States*, Table 759: 'Persons below poverty level by state: 1980 to 1998,' www.census.gov/prod/ 2001pubs/statab/sec14.pdf.

— (2008) *Statistical Abstract of the United States*, www.census.gov/ compendia/statab/.

US Department of Health and Human Services – Administration for Children and Families (1999) *Change in Welfare Caseloads*, January, www.acf.dhhs.gov/news/ stats/caseload.htm.

US Personal Responsibility and Work Opportunity Reconciliation Act (1996) P.L. 104-193.

Waldron, J. (1997) 'Homelessness and the issue of freedom,' in R. E. Gooding and P. Pettit (eds), *Contemporary Political Philosophy*, Oxford: Blackwell.

Wertheimer, A. (1996) *Exploitation*, Princeton, NJ: Princeton University Press.

White, S. (2007) *Equality*, Cambridge: Polity Press.

Winstanley, G. (2006) *The Law of Freedom and Other Writings*, ed. C. Hill, Cambridge: Cambridge University Press.

Wolff, E. N. (2004) 'Changes in household wealth in the 1980s and 1990s in the U.S.,' Working Paper 407, Levy Economics Institute of Bard College.

Wolff, R. P. (1970) *In Defense of Anarchism*, New York: Harper & Row.

Wood, E. M. (1995) *Democracy against Capitalism: Renewing Historical Materialism*, Cambridge: Cambridge University Press.

— (1999) *The Origins of Capitalism*, New York: Monthly Review Press.

Wright, E. O. (1997) *Class Counts: Comparative Studies in Class Analysis*, Cambridge: Cambridge University Press.

— (2006) 'Compass points: towards a socialist alternative,' *New Left Review*, 41.

Zafirovski, M. (2003) 'Measuring and making sense of labor exploitation in contemporary society: a comparative analysis,' *Review of Radical Political Economics*, 35.

Index

Abraham Lincoln Battalion, 118
African National Congress (ANC),
    118–20
agriculture: settled, 22; subsistence,
    23
Althusser, Louis, 122
anarchism, 44, 47, 83, 87–95, 106;
    critique of state, 88
Anderson, Benedict, 109, 122
Angola, 119
aristocracy, 86
Aristotle, 16, 25; *The Politics*, 25
Athens city state, 18–19, 24, 36;
    democracy in, 103–4

Bakunin, Mikhail, 88, 89
banks, collapse of, 130
Baptists, 9
Bebel, August, 114
Bellamy, Edward, *Looking
    Backward*, 21, 39, 60, 64, 72, 78,
    82
benefits, social, elimination of, 125–7
Berlin, Isaiah, 40, 46
Bernstein, Eduard, 66
Bismarck, Otto von, 75
Bolshevik Revolution, 116
borders of political community,
    drawing of, 108
bourgeoisie, 113, 121–2
budget cutting, 76

California, ballot initiative in, 107
capitalism, 23, 27; property
    ownership in, 22
Carter, Jimmy, 76
centrally planned economies, 61–2,
    63, 74
China, 1

Cicero, *Republic*, 36
citizenship, 111; definition of, 96–7;
    inclusive, 98
class and class struggles, 21–31
Clinton, Bill, health plan, 76
coercion, 51
Cohen, G. A., 12, 17, 48, 79
Cold War, 6, 99
collective bargaining, 68
collective ownership, 63; of means of
    production, 65, 67
Cominel, George, 13
Comintern, 121
commons *see* privatization, of
    commons
communism, 2, 3, 4, 9, 27, 34, 65, 111
Communist League, 12
Communist Party of the United
    States, 117
community of equals, 81–2
conservatism, 5
credit card debt, 130
crime, 39; violent, related to
    inequality, 89
Crosland, Anthony, 66
Crusoe, Robinson, 40
cultural identity, politics of, 133

Dahl, Robert, 98
Darwin, Charles, 27
democracy, 36, 63, 83–107; direct,
    106–7; in ancient Athens, 103; in
    ancient Greece, 25; participatory,
    104, 107; political outcomes in,
    103; social egalitarian, 99–107
democratic centralism, 105
Devine, James, 54
Diamond, Jared, 17–18, 21–2; *Guns,
    Germs, and Steel*, 14

Diggers, 38–9
distribution: of goods, 35; of
    income, 75; of opportunities,
    70; of productive property, 58;
    of resources, 39, 50, 69, 70; of
    wealth, 30–1, 40, 42
division of labour, 15–16, 17, 19

economic crisis, 62
economy, and society, 49–82
education, 50–1; as public good, 71
egalitarianism, 4
eight-hour working day, 80
electronic benefits transfer (EBT),
    127
enclosures, 37
Engels, Friedrich, 25, 27, 66, 109,
    122, 130
England, as despot of world market,
    113
equality, 34–40, 43, 69; material, 70;
    of freedom, 34–48; of income, 69
Executive of the Communist
    International, 117
exploitation, 51–9; eliminating
    causes of, 59–67; modifying
    effects of, 67–81

Fanon, Frantz, 119
feudalism, 17, 22, 36–7, 55, 131
financial crisis, 130–2
financial instruments, proliferation
    of, 129
Foley, Duncan, 13, 54
forces of production,
    revolutionization of, 28
Fourier, Charles, 45, 77–8; *The
    Theory of the Four Movements*,
    39
free choice, nature of, 46
free time: distribution of, 81; need
    for, 77–9
free-riding, problem of, 94
freedom, 40–8; equality of,
    34–48; individual, loss of, 81;

maximization of, 102; negative,
    40, 42, 45, 46, 69, 71, 93–4;
    positive, 93–4
Friedman, Milton, 40, 46–7, 49, 52,
    66, 71, 90

Germany: role in revolution, 116;
    slave labour in, 20
Giuliani, Rudolph, 128–9
globalization, 123; and labor market,
    121; of capitalism, 113–14
Goldman, Emma, 87, 88, 93
Gorbachev, Mikhail, 100
Gould, Stephen Jay, 28
government, 94, 103; absence of, 86;
    not optional, 83; value of, 85–6
government regulation, rollback of,
    129
government service, pay for, 104
Gramsci, Antonio, 116
Great Depression, 26, 27, 130
Greece, ancient, 36
Greenspan, Alan, 130
guaranteed minimum income, 125
Guérin, Daniel, 92
Gutnov, Alexei, 73–4

Hartz, Louis, 131
health and safety, 102
health insurance, 126
healthcare, 71; in USA, 1–2, 71, 76–7
Herder, Johann Gottfried von, 109
Hervé, Gustave, 114
hierarchy, 37–8
historical materialism, 6–33; and
    political philosophy, 31–3
history: materialist view of, 8–14;
    theory of, 7
Hobbes, Thomas, 6–7, 25, 43, 56, 59;
    Leviathan, 37–8, 84–6, 87
Hobsbawm, Eric, 29, 109–10
Hoover, Herbert, 21
housing, 74
hunting and gathering economies,
    15, 20, 22

ideological interpellation, 122
income distribution *see* distribution of income
individual qualities, difference of, 35
Industrial Revolution, 18, 26, 39, 80
industrialization, 19, 62; of USSR, 80
inequality, 51; in US, 29–30; legitimacy of, 42; of income, 3
International Brigades, 117–18, 121
internationalism, 5, 108–24; as ideology, 120–4; as lived practice, 118
invisible hand, 42
Irish question, 111–12
isogoria, 36
isonomia, 36
isotimia, 36

Kamenev, Lev, 117
Kautsky, Karl, 115
Khrushchev, Nikita, 100
kibbutz: equality in, 81; ethics of, 69
King, Martin Luther, 132
Kropotkin, Peter, *Mutual Aid*, 89

labor, contractual, 16
labor market, 26, 27, 30, 51, 59, 67, 68, 75, 80, 93, 107; and globalization, 121; rights of, 68
Labour Party (UK), 66
law, necessity of, 96
leisure activities, pursuit of, 44–5
lemonade stand capitalism, 128
Lenin, V. I., 66, 105–6, 115–16; *State and Revolution*, 106
liberalism, 40, 41, 42–3, 45, 49, 50, 56, 63, 70, 91, 94, 97
Locke, John, 37, 56–7; *Second Treatise of Government*, 7
Luxemburg, Rosa, 115

Madison, James, 25
Mandela, Nelson, 118
Manuel, Trevor, 120
market, 63, 90; as coordinator of

scarce resources, 49; as model of economic democracy, 63; failure of, 72; global, 112; rationing of commodities, 77; regulation of, 72
market fundamentalism, 5
Marshall, T. H., 2, 75, 125
Marx, Karl, 6, 25, 45, 53, 65, 70, 77–9, 82, 87, 97, 103, 105, 106, 109, 122, 130; *Capital*, 54, 78; *Critique of Political Economy*, 10–11, 17, 27; *Critique of the Gotha Programme*, 113; *Economic and Philosophical Manuscripts*, 44; theory of history, 6; with Friedrich Engels (*Communist Manifesto*, 1, 12, 60–1, 62, 99, 110, 115; *The German Ideology*, 120)
mass parties, foundation of, 26
materialist theory of history, 133
Mayo, James, 73
Mazzini, Giuseppe, 110
Mbeki, Thabo, 120
means of production *see* collective ownership of means of production
Meidner, Rudolf, 61
Mill, John Stuart, *On Liberty*, 97
modes of production, 29, 33
monarchy, 6, 38
monastery, equality in, 81
monopoly of resources, 23
More, Thomas, 82; *Utopia*, 38, 41, 69, 72, 78–9, 81
Mormons, 9
mortgage market, 129–30

nation-state, 112, 120, 123; as political inventions, 108; political transcendence of, 109
nationalism, 109–10, 111, 119
nationalization of industries, 102
neoliberalism, 129
New Economic Policy, 66

newspaper, reading of, 122–3
Nimtz, August, 99
Novye Elementy Rasseleniia, 73–4
Nozick, Robert, 42

Obama, Barack, 1–2
Orwell, George, *Nineteen Eighty-Four*, 76
ownership, 19; rules of, 22

Pan-Africanism, 110
Paris Commune, 105–6, 112–13
Parks, Rosa, 132
Parti Ouvrier Français, 75
patriotism, international, 115
Personal Responsibility and Work Opportunity Reconciliation Act (PRA) (USA), 125, 128
Plato, *Republic*, 24
political emancipation, 95–8
political leadership, role of, 11
political philosophy, 5, 7, 13, 32, 35, 42, 72, 84, 89; and historical materialism, 31–3; study of, 3
politics, as a range of processes, 8
postmodernism, 133
poverty, 128; reduction of, 126–7, 129
prices, determination of, 53
private property, 7, 40, 49, 56–7, 67, 68, 72, 87–8, 90, 98; abolition of, 38, 65; power of, 98; protection of, 97, 103; state support of, 94–5
privation state, 125–34
privatization, of commons, 37, 38
production, primacy of, 15
productive forces, ownership of, 16
productivity, increases in, 79–80
profit, 52–4, 64, 79, 80; abstinence theory of, 53
property: as productive capital, 58; conflict over rights of, 25; productive, monopolization of, 87 *see also* private property
property rights, 97; defense of, 91; enforcement of, 84

Proudhon, Pierre-Joseph, 86, 90
Przeworski, Adam, 101
public goods, 74; rationing of, 77; supply of, 72–3, 76, 94
public ownership, of industry, 60
public space, 73
public transportation, 73
publicly owned enterprises, 20

Rand, Ayn, 83
Reagan, Ronald, 76
recession, 62
Red Cross packages, reallocation of, 49–50
reformism, 66
Reiman, Jeffrey, 89
relations of production, 16–17, 24, 32
resources, access to, 69
revolution, 11, 12, 25; American, 38; national, 112; of 1848, 12; Russian, 19, 99–100, 116
right to strike, 67
rights: legal, 2; political, 2; social, 2, 3, 75
Robinson Crusoe, 46
Rome, ancient, 36
Roosevelt, Franklin D., 21, 46
Rousseau, Jean-Jacques, 6, 11, 14, 82, 97; *Discourse on the Origins of Inequality*, 9–10, 43; *The Social Contract*, 7, 104–5

Sassoon, Donald, 69
scientific research, status of, 64
Seattle protests, 120, 121
Second International, 114, 117, 121
self-interested human nature, 42, 43, 44
self-rule, 97; legitimacy of, 95–6
Sen, Amartya, 69
Shaw, George Bernard, 69
slavery, 10, 20, 22, 23, 38, 51
Smith, Adam, 32, 37, 41, 42, 67, 90, 109; *Wealth of Nations*, 7, 15–16, 58

social democracy, 4, 9, 34
Social Democratic Party (Germany), 99
Social Democratic Party (Sweden), 61
Social Democratic Workers' Party (Germany), 113
social egalitarianism, 5, 13, 34, 43, 45, 47, 51, 60, 62, 63, 67, 69, 70, 72, 80, 81, 91, 95, 99–107, 108, 133; in USA, 131; relation to democracy, 102–3
social insurance scheme, in Germany, 75
socialism, 2, 3–4, 9, 26, 47, 66, 83, 100–2, 130; foreign in America, 131; in Europe, 99; in one country, 117; utopian, 39
Socrates, 24–5
solidarity: international, 110, 115; working-class, 109
Sombart, Werner, 131
South Africa, resistance to apartheid in, 118–20
sovereignty, 104, 110
Spanish Civil War, 117–18
Sparta city state, 18–19
Stalin, Joseph, 100, 117, 121
state: anarchist critique of, 83–4; coercive force of, 86; distorting influence of, 92; elimination of, 93; role of, 68, 72 (in USA, 27); society without, 86–95 *see also* anarchist critique of state *and* privation state
state power, 84–6
stateless societies, 18
Stockman, David, 76
subsistence crops, 23
surplus, economic, 21; appropriation of, 16
surplus value, 54
Sweden, 21
Szporluk, Roman, 111

technological innovation, 26, 64
Thatcher, Margaret, 76
Therborn, Goran, 122
Third International, 116
Trotsky, Leon, 115
Turner, Frederick Jackson, 131

unemployment, 68
Union of Soviet Socialist Republics (USSR), 19, 63, 73–4, 117, 119; formation of, 99–101; performance of economy of, 67
United States of America (USA), 2–3, 19, 21, 99, 102; constitution of, 125; economic crisis in, 1; health insurance in, 34; imports and exports of, 108; inequality in, 29–30; productivity in, 30; role of government intervention in, 27; social welfare in, 75; wealth gap in, 129; welfare state in, 125–6
universal membership, 109
utopianism, 43, 44

value: distinct from price, 54; labor theory of, 55; theory of, 55
voluntary association, 93; principle of, 90, 92
vote: restriction of, 97; right to, 96
voter participation rates, in USA, 107

wage labor, 52
wages of workers, 69, 79
welfare state, in USA, 125–6
Wigforss, Ernst, 82
Wilson, William Julius, 129
Wilson, Woodrow, 110
Winstanley, Gerrard, 38–9; *The Law of Freedom*, 39; *The New Law of Righteousness*, 39
Wolff, Robert Paul, 88
Wood, Ellen Meiksins, 13, 97
work process, control of, 30
workers: collective agreement among, 19–20; European,

rights of, 102; right to collective
bargaining, 21
workfare programs, 129
working hours: limitation of, 78, 80,
81, 99, 102; of British peasantry,
79

Zinoviev, Grigory, 117